Impressing the Whites

The New International Slavery

Richard Crasta

ISBN: 1469906295

ISBN-13: 978-1469906294

BOOKS BY RICHARD CRASTA

Richard Crasta, the author of *The Revised Kama Sutra: A Novel*, has been published in ten countries and in seven languages by more than twelve different publishers including Fourth Estate, U.K. Penguin, and HarperCollins.

Praise for *The Revised Kama Sutra: A Novel*

"Important ... and indictment of colonialism and the colonial legacy."— *The Hindu*
"Very funny" — Kurt Vonnegut
"Humorous and irrepressibly manic." — *The Independent*, UK
"Hilarious and delicate." — *The Face*, U.K.
"Indefatigable good humor . . . considerable charm." — *Publishers Weekly*

Other Books by Richard Crasta:

- *Beauty Queens, Children and the Death of Sex*
- *Fathers, Rebels, Dreamers* (editor, co-author)
- *What We All Need*
- *The Killing of an Author*
- *The Mahatma, the Goats, and Young Cats*

and other books on Amazon, Apple, Barnes & Noble, Kobo, Google Play, and Createspace.

.

ABOUT THIS EDITION

Though, over the years, the author has made minor edits to the book, the presiding principle has been to preserve the book's original flavor and passion, and to not let post-publication doubts or afterthoughts, including political correctness or historical developments, blight the fresh and inspired language of the original; like Jacques Derrida, the author believes that *once something is written, it is written, and must be respected for giving voice to that moment in time, its mood, its particular circumstances.* The author believes that the major, underlying principles in this book are still true to a large extent and that this book will make many readers question their assumptions.

The author considers the Glossary, Footnotes, Notes, and the Author's Disclaimer to be integral parts of the book, parts that will help in the fuller appreciation of the whole.

CONTENTS

AUTHOR'S DISCLAIMER

Any resemblance to real persons or books living or murdered is purely coincidental. *Void where fatwahed, and fatwahed almost everywhere.* Some assembly of facts and intelligence required. Batteries not included. Contents may settle during reading or as a result of heavy drinking. Use only as directed; *misuse permitted only to critics who have made up their minds before reading this book.* Do not read while operating a motor vehicle or a *vibrator.* Little Ayatollahs not yet proven to be blood relations of the original Ayatollah.

The "facts" in this book, indeed any statement in this book, have no bearing on any fact, living or dead. Any resemblance is a regrettable oversight and will be remedied with the next edition or by year's end, at which point this book will automatically self-destruct.

Further, in buying this book, you agree that you are purchasing just this book — and not its author. The author reserves the right to revise, reissue, rethink, or repudiate his book, and to sell his pet flea into slavery if offered a fair price.

This book combines satire with truthful, passionate, sincere, and idealistic observations — a unique mix that has been a trademark of the author's writing (though more so in some books than in others). It is against any form of racial typecasting. *Indeed, the author was helped by sincere, idealistic white persons of integrity in the editing and launching of this book,* and wishes to emphasize that in most cases, "whites" — a term used for convenience, as a kind of shorthand — refers to the power structure that often oppresses powerless whites and colored alike. This book being in the satirical tradition of Jonathan Swift, Mark Twain, and Ambrose Bierce, it would weaken the writing to repeatedly qualify one's statements. Therefore, anyone quoting individual lines out of context, without irony, without acknowledging this statement, and with an intention to mislead others should have his or her height *or head* examined.

DEDICATION

To the late James Baldwin, Ralph Ellison, Richard Wright — and to all other colored writers who tell it like it is, and who do it with style and soul and great courage.

THE BAD BOY'S CONTRITE PREFACE
& The Nigeria Shell Factor In Publishing

I am a bad boy. I confess this right away, in the time-honored Bad Boys Anonymous fashion, so that is settled. I tried in the last few years to be good. I tried to pretend I was not bad, but it simply wouldn't work: at odd, unguarded moments, the bad boy would stick his coconut out and say, "Yoo hoo! It's me!"

Let me clarify: I have never indulged in rape, torture, serial murders, or panty raids; never have I invaded countries, used chemical weapons, or tested hydrogen bombs in other people's backyards. I have spilled not a single fellow human's blood. To the charges of having murdered about twenty flies, more than two thousand mosquitoes, and about three hundred ants, I plead guilty, but take the hygiene, self-defense, or temporary insanity defenses respectively. I could try, but might never come up to the Real Life Bad Boy standards set by John Cheever, Celine, menage-a-troised Kingsley Amis, menage-a-zillioned Marquis De Sade, Catullus, Charlie Chaplin, Andre Gide, five-wived John Osborne and Saul Bellow, four-wived Salman Rushdie, multi-mistressed Robert Crumb and Robert Graves, and polymorphously perverse Anais Nin (one of the boys, if you pardon my saying so).

You see, I am only — or mostly — a *literary* bad boy, in the tradition of H.L. Mencken, Mark Twain, D.H. Lawrence, Lawrence Durrell and Hunter Thompson, though I am merely one of the humbler practitioners of this genre.

So why did I try to rein in this now-fashionable literary naughtiness that is an integral part of my voice and nature, not merely a modish put-on? Because I heeded all those — my agent included

— who warned me (though not in so many words): "Sssssshhh! Be careful! No Third World bad boys allowed!"

Until I came to America, I had never thought of my color or my race as a liability. Indeed, I am such a true One-Worlder that I wish we could banish such dehumanizing ways of categorizing people as ethnic origins and physical appearances. Nor do I believe that any color has a monopoly on suffering and invisibility (the present book was produced with the help of three American writers of European ancestry, all of whom related to some humanity in my writing). But eighteen years of living in the West have taught me to hate the color of my skin. It never seems to tell the right story about me, and most often tells stories that are infuriating and insulting. Short of handing out a brochure or a short book called *Me, My Skin, and My Complete Ethnic & Post-Ethnic History*, how could I explain to a Westerner who sees me (more often, not-sees me) that I am not an "Indian," a Middle-Easterner, a Hispanic, or a terrorist, but an exile without a country?

So, after having, in the first edition of my novel, *The Revised Kama Sutra*, flouted the rules of literary apartheid by creating an unapologetic and sexually swaggering protagonist instead of a submissive and monkey-trick-playing suitable brown boy, I began to back off a tiny bit. I now see that this suppression of my true, Vishnu-given bad-boy nature in the hope of a little green from the white gods — just so that they might pick me up, deposit me on their laps, pet me, and say, "Suitable Baby! Koochi koochi koo!" — was a betrayal of my true self, the cause of the depression that has made me make strategic mistakes and spend nearly a decade in unproductive mournfulness. Yes, I, a writer who had written what the Viking India jacket described as "one of the funniest novels to come out of India," was becoming a Sad Sack. At times, even I couldn't stand my funereal company.

But since there are too few of us Third World literary bad boys in existence, and too few who can afford to be bad boys — though our history gives us every cause — we carry an extra burden to forswear all goodness, all suitability. And so, besides being an essay on mind control and literary apartheid, this book is a combined birth announcement, sampler, excerpt, manifesto, and act of self-expression that could not be postponed for one more day. To hell with perfectionism, to hell with the veiled warnings, to hell with the pompous advice of the Literary Pundits (professional as well as those who have never read a book since they left high school) who would have me bang or wring out another novel "better" than the last one — and suppress my bursting heart until then. I had to write this book to save my soul, to exorcise my personal ghosts, to expel the poisons that have been eating into my vitals. And I have to do it *now*, without further ado. I cannot do this without taking the risk that I might be wrong, and occasionally repetitive.

Besides, as I just read in Ron Howard's *Mystic Path to Cosmic Power*, which is certainly not the worst book I have ever picked up from a motel library, "you must stop living so timidly, from fixed fears of what others will think of you, and what you will think of yourself." I really could do with a little Cosmic Power.

Still, I recognize that this conflict and my lonely crusade for literary justice may have not been the best route to health and happiness. Though I am an Indian with no sacred cows whatsoever, I have, from time to time, become attracted to some of the holistic, one-world, non-confrontational Eastern philosophies, in which all conflict (or rape, or murder) is illusory, immaterial, simply a misunderstanding or conceptual error. I would love nothing more than to deny my perception that the Western publishing world operates by double standards as colonialist and destructive to formerly colonial peoples as the behavior of Royal Dutch Shell in Nigeria, which Greenpeace accused of murdering a few leading members of the local tribes opposing the company's profitable operations. In this post-colonial *modus operandi*, accommodating locals are found, patronized, and propped up, and rebels and "troublemakers" eliminated, sometimes with the help — conscious or unconscious — of the accommodating locals themselves. And I say this post-Arundhati-Roy, yet with a wisdom gleaned from pre-Arundhati-Roy days, and also before I had read James Baldwin's *The*

Fire Next Time: The literary hospitality and fairness of the Western world is subordinate to the overwhelming Western agenda that is the neutering of the Third World male.

To deny this takes place is only to postpone facing the truth. For years, tweed-jacketed American intellectuals and blow-dried talking heads have denied the continued existence of racism in America (including their own; after all, some of their favorite actors, musicians, sports stars, and film mammies were black). Pointing to cultural icons such as Bill Cosby, Michael Jackson, and Oprah Winfrey, they could ignore the huge subterranean racial divide affecting the overwhelming majority of black people, until the Los Angeles riots and the O.J. Simpson trial aftermath briefly woke them up (following which they returned to being the United States of Amnesia). In Britain, where an ex-brown Rushdie is intellectual King [or was, in 1996, when this was originally written], the Guinness-sozzled atmosphere in some of the posher pubs (I adore British pubs) seems as universalistic and brotherly as a utopian's dream, and talk of literary apartheid and mental colonialism might sound quaint to some.

To tell the truth, it also sounds quaint to millions of Indians, newly inducted into the World Fraternity of the Boob-Tube-Smitten by "Friends" or MTV Asia, thanks to which a Benetton Colors Utopia of the Cathode Ray Tube reigns. And so it did to a couple of Indian university professors who, after my talk to their students, monopolized the discussion time and didn't once give their student sheep a chance to speak, practicing colonialism on them the way it had once been practiced on me. As for the modish-liberal Western magazines, their attitude seems to be: For heaven's sake, man, it's a post-colonialist, compassion-fatigued, celebrity-worshiping age. And all every member of the Diana-loving human family wants is cheap jeans and the chance to watch the Oscar ceremonies and cabled Disney. Right?

Well, examine the case presented in the following pages: that this book is not just, or not even mainly, about one book and one writer, but about nothing less than the dignity of a one-billion-strong chunk of humankind (and by extension, that of the four billion earthlings of the darker-hued persuasion who suffer from some of the same disabilities and restrictions): and therefore, about justice, free expression, self-determination, and diversity. In other words, a perfect illustration of the statement: the personal is the political.

Of course, this personal-political book is intimately connected with another semi-bad, ex-bad boy, Salman Rushdie. He wins a guest-starring role in this book (not the Booker again, sorry, old boy!), because he symbolizes the Third World's predicament. It is an indictment of our foolish politics that here was a writer who partially broke the shackles of colonial linguistic repression and dared to question his Makers — only to be imprisoned by his need to be protected by the West, and thus to be forced to defend his defenders, even to *become* them. The very novel that was the strongest statement of his political independence spelled the end of it. In a recent review, he, the once subversive writer, praised a book as "responsible." Ah, heavy burden! Well, this is my last responsible book, Salman; I find they take too much work. After this, I shall writing nothing but *irresponsible* books.

For as I know, and as you the reader better know (if you care): we bad brown boys are an endangered species, far more so than the African ape, the civet cat, or the now-thriving bald eagle, with no government or even a small-town arts organization committed to saving us from extinction. And there's a price on our heads, with the "well-behaved" brown boys chipping in their loot to raise the bounty. You might as well treasure us while we're still around. For every good country needs a few bad boys and bad girls, and there's no saying what might become of us once we have surrendered our souls to bland chicken soup (the inspirational series, now an international publishing empire which seems to crowd out indigenous authors and thinking in many Asian bookstores) and our bodies to McDonaldsized cuisine.

PART I: WHITE? ALL RIGHT

Generally speaking, Negro writing in the past has been confined to humble novels, poems, and plays, prim and decorous ambassadors who went a-begging to white America. They entered the Court of American Public Opinion dressed in the knee-pants of servility, curtsying to show that the Negro was not inferior, that he was human, and that he had a life comparable to that of other people. For the most part these artistic ambassadors were received as though they were French poodles who do clever tricks.

— Richard Wright, "Blueprint for Negro Writing"

[Langston Hughes] and his fellow artists intended to express their "individual dark-skinned selves without fear or shame. If white people are pleased we are glad . . . If colored people are pleased we are glad. If they are not, their displeasure doesn't matter either."

— David Levering Lewis, Introduction, The Viking Portable Harlem Renaissance Reader

IMPRESSING THE WHITES: THE
INTERNATIONAL DYNAMICS OF RACE TODAY

It was a nippy, late-August evening in that ancient capital of Scotland, Edinburgh. I was puffing uphill towards Edinburgh Castle and the setting sun, my tired feet trudging over the thousand-year-old stone-paved road called the Royal Mile, my mood anything but regal. Then I saw a sign that lifted my sagging spirits. "Indian brasserie," it said, which I first misread as "brassiere."

Proceeding bravely in the direction of the sign, I little suspected that in this pub-rich Scottish capital, where I was winding down the low-profile publicity tour for my novel *The Revised Kama Sutra*, I would be the beneficiary of semi-divine Enlightenment — even if it were not in the same class as the one that had greeted my countryman Buddha at the end of his eight-year stay in the forest. For in this Indian "brasserie," or curry shop with atmospheric enhancements, I met an Indian immigrant, a butter-faced businessman whom I will call Ashok the Hun. Having noticed that touristy Indian schlock and the usual quasi-spiritual merchandise glittered attractively behind the large display window of his trinketry-cum-eatery, I decided to get to know him a bit. This would be a prelude to my gently suggesting that he help promote my novel, a subversive and politically provocative novel which had not even been reviewed at that point, let alone burned, banned, or stomped on by jackbooted skinheads or even by the odd, miscast, camel-loving fundamentalist. If there had been the slightest intention in my mind to try to suggest to him that he display five copies of my book in his store window, to lounge in the odd company of joss sticks and bottles of Ayurvedic snake oil, then it must have been a product of extreme fatigue.

Pleased that I had introduced myself, Ashok the Hun began telling me his life story, or rather, his Amazing Success Story. He was casually joined by a chap who must have listened to this story a million times: his soul partner and business buddy, Ahmed.

"Three years ago, I came here, I was sweeping floors. I went hungry for three days, I lost three pounds!" said Ashok.

Really? You probably needed it, you ghee-fed prick.

He continued: "Sweeping floors! Sweeping *floors!* In India, I was a chaudhury [a member of the powerful landowner caste]! I had *eleven* servants! I didn't even touch *my own* shoes. And then I came here ... and one day, I was using a Hoover machine! *I, a Chaudhuri, using a Hoover machine like a chaparasi, you understand?!*" He paused for effect and smiled. "Now, I own this!"

"*Own* this?" I asked, impressed. *You fat cat, you.*

"I manage the entire building."

"Oh, I see." *He had the authority to kick someone out for peeing in the elevator.* Delicately changing the subject, I asked our mini-mogul, shyly, "Er, what would you think of investing in my novel?" I showed him my British hardcover. Dominating the center of its revisionist front jacket, a tiny and semi-demurely semi-covered but giddily ecstatic Marilyn Monroe was absorbed in a somewhat passionate and improbable pelvic embrace with a pleased-looking Mughal gentleman, their middles tightly wrapped in loud clothing, possibly to prevent the transmission of social diseases such as miscegenation.

"I'll tell you what," he said after a minute, conspiratorially, as if he were buying a consignment of damaged potatoes on the cheap. "You print ten thousand copies, and you have my name on the jacket to say I sponsored it. And *I'll* sell the book through my contacts. We'll make a huge profit."

At this point his partner Ahmed interjected, "No, no, have his *photo* on the jacket." Breaking out into laughter, he continued, "Arre, have the photo of his *big thing* on the jacket!"

I smiled, and barely restrained myself from asking Ahmed how he had ascertained the size of Ashok's penis, or how *big* was "big."

"Well, my name and my photo," continued Ashok the Hun, quite seriously. "How much you charge for ten thousand copies?"

Surprised by this sudden and unexpected question, and making a hurried but inaccurate mental calculation — seven pounds per book — I said, "Seventy thousand pounds." It seemed a fair offer, for at the time, I had no idea of the real cost of printing and book production in Western countries. I reckoned the total production costs would be forty thousand pounds, leaving me with thirty thousand as minimally acceptable remuneration for my six years of mostly unpaid literary labors.

His eyes popped. Seventy thousand pounds could purchase a heck of a lot of Hoovers, or cheap handloom shirts, or brass ashtrays from Chandni Chowk, after all.

"I'll tell you what," interjected Ahmed, who seemed to be on a roll. "You have to add twenty pages of photos. Without photos, people will be disappointed. I tell you what: *you write about gays and lesbians making love. It will be a big seller!*"

I laughed, realizing that my brief fantasy of a business deal was over. Still, I decided, purely as an intellectual exercise to occupy a dull evening with, to give him a bit of my spiel: the importance of Indians being able to publish courageous books, how this whole affair was a matter of our dignity and pride, as Indians, and perhaps even of our manhood: our right to stand up and express ourselves loudly and clearly, without censorship or inhibition, in any style or form we wished — goals that were beyond monetary valuation.

"If you have to talk to *us* about it, then you don't believe in the book," said Ashok, not entirely without logic. "You impress the *whites*, then you have made it. In this country, miracles can and do happen. In India and Pakistan, miracles *never* happen."

Impressing the Whites: a crudely expressed formula or insight, perhaps, but one that he, and others before him, had doubtlessly expressed before in their private circles, where there was no need to hold one's tongue and circumcise one's speech — because there was no need to, ahem, impress the whites. Not only had this thought been expressed, but it had most certainly been the formula that fueled the lives of thousands, millions, perhaps nearly a billion darker-skinned earthlings — the last number including those who practiced it unconsciously.

Nothing, nothing, nothing at all is quite wasted on a writer, or need be. Without quite realizing it, Ashok the Hun, or rather Ashok the Rough Diamond, as I renamed him over the next few months, had more than helped me with my literary career. Had I been a Greek philosopher, I might have run out into the Edinburgh streets, stark naked, shouting, "Eureka! Eureka!" For Ashok had been midwife to an understanding that had been latent within me; he had in fact delivered into my hands the title and an idea for an entire book. It was a book whose writing and necessity — its inevitability, if I valued my integrity — would obsess me over the next five years through rewrites and more rewrites as I consciously pondered a phenomenon that was lodged deep in the heart of brownness, of darkness of skin, of the international order of melanin.

Impressing the whites. Impressing the whites even to get the faintest validation for our humanity. Impressing the whites, period. The story of our miracle-starved lives, of too many Indian and Third World lives, whether we be like the culturally barren Ashok the Huns yearning for materialistic success and emigration; whether we be Bombayites trying to put on Oxford accents and fake a knowledge of cheeses and wines; or whether we be Delhi literati striving to make a favorable impression on Delhi's Western diplomats [see Endnote] — minor potentates who have, either by their power to throw parties and patronize locals and soak 'em up with Scotch and grant them visas, favors, or cultural junkets, or by their personal charm, become resident reminders of the superiority and the power of the white race. Having stubbornly held onto my Indian passport all these years [which I did for seventeen years until 2000, when a divorce compelled me to acquire US citizenship so as to have unfettered access to my young children], I am not immune, as no brown skinned person trying to function in the larger world can be: I have to occasionally "impress the whites" to get my passport stamped with short-stay European tourist visas.

How pervasive is this phenomenon? So pervasive, in fact, that a cursory examination of Indian bestseller lists suggests that virtually no *literary* book by an Indian writer working in English will make it really big in demi-white enclaves such as Bombay unless it impresses the hell out of the whites in London or New York. That's the new destiny, the new Promised Land, the new karma of the favorite sons of Mother Ganga — and has been, particularly since the mid-nineteenth century, when Lord Macaulay, smuggling in Occidental arrogance and condescension under the guise of educating the natives, dealt the *coup de gräce* to an already battered Indian self-confidence. Indian poet and mahatma,[1] Rabindranath Tagore, complained that Indians became aware of his existence only *after* he had won the Nobel Prize; and then they became insufferably, intrusively sycophantic. Even the Ultimate Mahatma himself, Mohandas Karamchand Gandhi, was accepted as an Indian leader only after he had impressed the whites in South Africa, and as a world leader only after he had impressed the liberal whites in America and England, whose batting for him was an essential factor in Britain's change of heart, its realization that giving up the Crown of the Empire was inevitable. (It is a pity that Gandhi did not impress those on the Nobel Committee, as Richard Wright, Ralph Ellison, and James Baldwin did not, but Salman Rushdie might). What a yogic feat, what a giant leap for one of the world's oldest, greatest, and philosophically exalted cultures: from the sublime destiny of becoming one with Brahman, from escaping the cycle of *maya* and rebirth, to the rather pedestrian, crass one of impressing the whites in our lives — the live white persons who wear suits and skirts, as well as the White Superegos inside our heads.

* * *

Inside our heads? Yes, I suggest that this impressively powerful

---

[1] Great soul.

formula has taken control of our internal command centers, that perhaps hundreds of millions of us Indians are guilty of going blue in the face trying to impress the whites. Indeed, I will go further and say that we have surrendered our souls to white *worship* — and also to black hatred, yellow hatred, and self-hatred, which seem often to be the secret confederates of white worship (there is a shade of this in Sir V.S. Naipaul, a super-successful Niradh Chaudhuri who reinvented himself as an Englishman, having washed away some of his melanin with a combination of genius and determination). Inside our heads, Indian civilization has been defeated by Western values and materialism. Yes! *Inside our heads!* That is why, nearly half a century after independence, Indian editors nervously awaited the results of Britain's Booker Prize as if these were the results of India's sovereign national elections rather than of their ex-colonial oppressor Britain's appointment, as it turned out, of the Literary King-Emperor of India.[2] Even though Vikram Seth, author of that Super Big Mac of a novel, *The Suitable Boy,* did not ultimately win the prize, his emperorship was assured by a million-dollar advance and the British media hoopla that he had already received. And most Indians, despite internal doubts and prompts of "This is worth a million? This is our best? You must be kidding!" responded with cries of "Hail! All Hail King Vikram!" — with the gray-haired doyen of Indian journalism, megacolumnist Khushwant Singh, leading the chorus like a dutiful vizier.

Like many nonwhite former colonies that continue to allow Her Majesty the British Queen to appoint their Governor Generals, we in our curious snootiness still prefer British rule, not willing to give as much credence to the upstart Americans, who have given their imprimaturs to Dinesh D'Souza and Bharati Mukherjee. Our white worship, our genuflection before the Color White, is betrayed by the

---

[2] This chapter was written at the time that Vikram Seth, author of *A Suitable Boy,* was indeed accepted as the Literary King of India by India's English-language media. Guarded by the Cerberuses from Penguin India, which some would call the unofficial local Literary Office of the Empire, access to His Majesty by journalists of brown hue was strictly limited.

matrimonial advertisements in Indian papers (*"Wanted fair-complexioned groom for very fair-complexioned bride"*), and by the anxious efforts of many "successful" Indian immigrants in America to "become" white by making derogatory racist remarks about American blacks and joining the covertly racist Republican party.

Sometimes, the darker the relative color of our own skins, the harder we strain to reinvent ourselves to impress the whites. As a result, India is not just the world's largest democracy, being home also to the world's largest chunk of desperately poor people, but the world's largest producer of coconuts: persons who are brown on the outside, but white on the inside. And its GNCP (or Gross National Coconut Production) is increasing at a far more rapid pace than its GNP.

This wacky leucoderma, this Michael Jackson sickness, is not entirely the fault of our ex-rulers, the British, but partly the understandably human result of centuries of political, economic, and social domination by foreigners, starting with the devastating Muslim raids and conquests of the Eighth Century onwards, and perhaps even marginally in the Aryan invasions occurring two thousand years before Christ. As for the philistinism of modern-day India, which betrays its spiritual and artistic heritage by unashamed pursuit of materialism and discouragement of artistic endeavor (unless it results in tangible financial rewards, such as big advances and Booker Prizes), we are all damaged and made lesser human beings by it.

But selling out, aping Westerners, and pandering to Western expectations is what we Indians have been told we need to do to get ahead. The golden rule of Indian writers writing in English is this: *Do not fire your pen-guns until you hear the Ayes of the whites.* And we Indians, true children of Kautilya, the Indian Machiavelli, have become so adept at doing this that we can easily give lessons to other Third World races that may not be as sharp.

Laughing at my mention of the title of this book, and instantly understanding the book's essence, a Bangalore computer specialist I had just met on a domestic flight said to me, "It's something Indians are very good at." He added, almost as if the logical connection was obvious: "We have a *huge* inferiority complex."

One brilliant illustration of how powerfully this principle operates: the novels of the late Indrani Eknath Gyaltsen, an Indian woman writer who plagiarized two little-known British novels, changing only the names and the settings, were gobbled up by Western editors ravenously hungry to fill up their "Women and People of Color" quota — a Double Whopper for the price of a single.

Other Indian writers play more shrewdly to the white race, sometimes cultivating specific white godfathers, knowing that their lives could become very sweet indeed — million-dollar contracts, BBC-TV deals, invitations to writers' festivals, even the French treatment. I refer here to the treatment the French are in the habit of giving to visiting African dictators and cabinet ministers: an occasional sweet young thing lying naked on their beds instead of the chocolate mint under their pillows, a goodwill gift from a civilization rich in blonde sexpot goddesses to the starving representatives of the goddess-disadvantaged.

This Western carrot of acceptance and riches is accompanied by a stick: *Do not cross the boundaries. Always remember your place.* When my novel was circulating in the U.S. in manuscript form, I was warned against its insolent tone. I was advised by Western publishing insiders to simply take out a few provocative sentences and paragraphs — and perhaps, if I could, a chapter here, a naked editor there — and Fame would be mine. My manuscript had made it into the posh offices (and occasionally, the residences) of the famous and the powerful. I had received generous praise from some of them. All of this had swollen my head and made me feel stubborn and unstoppable. I didn't realize that most Indian writers never even get to my stage of receiving discreet warnings, because the carrot and stick are so discreetly transferred by Third World writers onto their *internal* censor that they are often unconscious of their own self-censorship. Foolishly inspired by Western literary and artistic martyrs who died starving for their principles (and subconsciously by the One who died on the Cross), I refused to edit out the daring parts, which I saw as making a *political* point for *Indians*.

The result, as any Third World writer who has tried to take such risks on behalf of his countrymen will tell you, is that you will rarely get any appreciation or thanks from your fellow Third World writers, who are too preoccupied with their own game of impressing the whites, and are irritated by any fellow-nationals' attempt to try something different, and who, on the contrary, are secretly thrilled to have one less competitor in the rat race to attract the attention and blessings of the All-Powerful White God.

* * *

At least the lower rungs of Indians in India have other Indians to strive to impress: their Indian bosses and the Indian rich. But upper-middle-class Indians have had white worship subtly ingrained in them. A senior Delhi-based Indian editor confessed to me, with frustration in his voice: "The foreigners who are posted here[3] are often very nice people when they arrive. But one year after they have been here [with Indians scrambling and fighting each other to please them and serve them because of the color of their skin] — they get spoiled." Meaning: they gradually begin to take their royal treatment and free multi-course meals for granted, socialize mostly with upper-class Indians, and after a while are even indignant when this special treatment is denied.

Even Indians in *India* know that in the larger scheme of things, it is the West that makes the rules. And they are pretty much resigned to it, as they are to summer and winter, day and night. Thus, when I first made the rounds of Delhi publishing houses between 1989 and 1990, asking if my novel-in-progress might interest them, their

---

[3] White Westerners who are posted in India on diplomatic or journalistic assignments. The name of this source: David Davidar, whose profound understanding of the way things operate in India has been proved, over time, to be superior to that of most others; this conversation occurred in 1994, when we were good friends.

automatic advice was: *Publish it in the West first.* Once you impress the Westerners — by being an immaculate ape of their best, safest writers, with Indian spices occasionally blended in for authenticity and local color — Indians will worship you. If you impressed *them,* you really must be good. Thus it is that even in India, it is the West that makes and breaks reputations, just as African filmmakers must depend on Western companies for distribution, affirmation, and survival.

* * *

It is understandable, then, that many a serious Third World writer with a message who sets out to write in English will discover, at some point, that he has no choice but to move to London or New York to "make it" as a writer, to find his potential audience, a large chunk of which exists in *other* Third World countries, where they can only be reached through media of international reach such as *Time, The Observer,* and *The Times Literary Supplement,* all controlled by Westerners. We in the Third World have gotten ourselves into such a mess, our heads and our distribution and financial systems so enslaved, that we can talk to each other only if the Sultans in London and New York permit us; even the Irish are honorary members of the Third World in that they too need to impress the London establishment if they are to make it in the U.S. and other international markets.

If this serious Third World writer writes without censoring his voice, however, he won't reach his potential audience, for the white gatekeepers will not let him. This is the new colonialism, the Nineties' change obviously way of subduing weaker people.

"India is a sovereign, independent country," you, the outraged, bewildered, or defensive Western reader say (yes, I must address You at times because it is only if You are Pleased and so Command that I will reach a sufficient number of Third World readers; though at this stage of the game, I will still say whatever I please). You ignore my hollow laugh and continue: "So why not say what you have to say in your own country? Why should *we* be interested?"

Well, because London is the capital of the venerable British Empire to which we are still mentally beholden, with Washington, New York, and Los Angeles being the ultimate, de facto super-capitals of the world. Drugged, softened, and helplessly addicted to Western television and its round-the-clock satellite-relayed buffet of brain-deadening pap, we have surrendered our four thousand years of cultural confidence, our old traditions of hospitality, where once a guest was welcomed with full attention and refreshments. We now offer a cool welcome to guests who arrive at our homes during the airing of the beach-bunny television serial *Baywatch*, and we often skip telling our children bedtime stories from *The Panchatantra* or *The Mahabharatha* lest we miss the evening's episode of that U.S.-rejected soap opera, *The Bold and the Beautiful*. Some of these newly colonized Indians are made nervous by incendiary writers among themselves, by the possible embarrassment they might feel when the Masters are offended, the possibility that their daily rations of brain dope may be cut off; they'll shout down fellow Indians for trying to speak on their behalf. They love their nooses, because nowadays, with modern technology and all, yaar, it's so luxurious, and it's made in *Hollywood*, baba!

And because, as I shall argue in the next chapter, it is a game in which a privileged class on each side of the East-West divide has something to gain, though at the expense of the majority.

THE OCCIDENTAL COW AND
THE NEW WORLD ORDER

As an unrepentantly Indian immigrant in my writings, with the label "Indian" pinned to my physiognomy whether or not I wish it, with my Indian birth determining my destiny and my movements in this fabulous world of the New World Order, I sometimes tend to write about my experiences and insights as if they related only to India. But the phenomenon of cultural and personal submission and subservience towards white people is a phenomenon without borders, as I have discovered in my travels through over forty countries, including Asian countries with Western expatriates or tourists as well as Western countries with nonwhite immigrants.

Indeed, I have observed Bangladeshi waiters, serving in allegedly "Indian" restaurants in Western cities, behaving in an even more servile manner towards white people than Indians do. India's controversial (and later, much regretted) invitation to Britain's Queen Elizabeth to preside over her former colony's *independence* anniversary was followed by a similar offer to Britain's Prince Charles by Sri Lanka to preside over its own independence celebrations. The invitations may have stemmed from an unconscious desire to demonstrate moral superiority or magnanimity, but in the process we forgot that our act of servility was the far greater sin than the remote possibility of being condemned as being "bitter"[4] about our colonial experience.

---

[4] As if "bitter" were not as much of an element of life (and of chocolate) as sweet, or of pungent and sour

Indeed, the phenomenon or the need to "impress the whites", to get the Gora Sahibs to pat us on our backs for our economic openness, our political freedoms, our fine morals, our willingness to sign the right treaties, or conversely, to have our enemies declared "terrorist states" by the Supreme Empire of the New White Order, America, extends in today's "post-colonial" world beyond South Asia into virtually every non-white country, including to a lesser degree Japan, which has never quite recovered from its Second World War defeat and its long and humiliating occupation by General MacArthur's troops. In *The Westernization of the World*, Serge Latrouche sees the "post-colonial" world as marching even more aggressively towards Westernization and colonization because "What is happening now seems much deeper and more lasting. The white man has gone offstage, while science, technology, and development have taken over. How can we de-colonize from that?"

I see the phenomenon as much deeper. In a purely cultural sense, people all over the non-Western world are going bananas. In countries hotter than hell, they bake and suffocate and choke themselves by wearing Western suits and neckties to impress the whites — and each other. They dress up or remodel not only tourist spots,[5] but entire countries and civilizations, substituting concrete roofs for natural tiles, confining formerly sun-kissed and oxygenated breasts and privates within industrial-strength bras and panties; abandoning their traditional hammock-cradles and breastfeeding practices in exchange for plastic and steel cribs and infection-prone infant formulas like Lactogen — all considered more modern and advanced and acceptable because they are made by corporations owned by the whites.

"Yes, Saar, Yes, Bwana, we have McDonalds, supermarkets, toilet paper, hot dogs, sandwiches, everything Western now, Sahib!"

---

[5] Including a Mysore restaurant named "The Empire", a Bangalore hotel named Windsor Manor, and an Indian restaurant in London that entices its customers to indulge their Inner Colonialist: "Relax in the atmosphere of colonial India!"

Billions of plastic bags, having retired the old reusable market bag, litter and clog the once pristine countryside and forests. Electrical transformers and satellite dishes scar the once-harmonious faces of many an ancient town. And surely, some visiting World Bank official will take note of these signs of "progress" and jot these countries down on his list of loan-worthy nations.

When I was working in a small town in the South Indian state of Karnataka, a few evangelically inclined white members of a California church made it known that they would like to pay a visit to the Archbishop of Bangalore, the state capital.. Bingo! The Archbishop swung into action. He mobilized his entire archdiocese and his schools to provide a VIP reception for these whites, who were ordinary middle-class citizens back in their hometowns. I don't mean to suggest that the Archbishop should have not been hospitable to people simply because they were middle-class citizens, only that the reception wouldn't have been one-fiftieth as royal for an Indian group of similar achievements. In fact, the Indian middle-class group would have been asked to wait outside and see the parish priest instead of the bishop. It is in this context that the reception was obscene and a ghastly lesson in deportment to the hundreds of brown parishioners and clergy whom the Archbishop had compulsorily enlisted in the task of bowing before the white delegation.

In New York, at a dinner party in an Indian home, if the solitary white guest were to ask a few deep and soulful questions, such as, "What is the dot on the Indian woman's head supposed to mean?" or "Aren't all Indians vegetarians?" or "Why are India and Pakistan always fighting?" or "So do you eat tandoori all the time?" all the vocal persons in the group will compete vociferously to provide an impressive answer to the visiting white — who is automatically deemed to be a superior being, even though there might be half a dozen Indians in the room with PhD degrees, while the white guest might not even have passed high school.

Whereas if you are the lone male brown person happening to find yourself in a party dominated by whites, it may happen that everyone except the host and perhaps one other kind liberal soul will ignore you and carry on with their chitchat, barely aware of your presence, making absolutely no attempt to include you in their conversation, let alone, heaven forbid, sinking so low as to try to impress you. You would be well advised, in these circumstances, to launch into a loud Vedic chant while doing a yogic headstand, or perhaps to take a dump in a large piece of crockery while performing the traditional 64-part ritual (well, Peter Sellers's portrayal of an Indian at a Hollywood party in *The Party* is right on in representing this sad situation; most Indians would be lucky to get one-quarter of his attention).

I say *male*, because an Indian woman attending such a party is the recipient of a goodly amount of attention under the Exotic Oriental Babe Exception, which I shall explain later.

* * *

What is the result of this New World Order, the modern avatar of the Old Colonial Order? Crown us a suitable boy, and we'll give you a million suitable boys and girls; we brown and yellow people exist only for Your pleasure, as You may have heard from all those heartwarming tourist brochures, in which happy and smiling yellow and brown waiters and waitresses welcome you to your luxurious hotels and spas (how come I see so few brochures of smiling white waiters welcoming brown and black guests to their luxurious hotels/). We exist, live, we breathe also for the occasional pat on the head *You* might be so pleased as to give us.

Consider the campaign in the Indian community to fund a Chair in Indian Studies at Columbia University: a noble cause in itself, one with which I have no quarrel whatsoever except in the context of what follows. As it happened, no less than $1.3 million had been collected at the time of this writing — a fortune, considering the emigrant Indian community's tightfistedness towards any *other* noble cause — meaning, any cause that is remotely intellectual or non-religious or non-Bollywood-filmi. And why? For all the high-minded platitudes favoring the cause, it won out over other meritorious causes because of one not-so-benign element: that here we Indians were, going in a delegation to Them, the Powers That Be, and pleading, "Please, please, say the words. Say them *India is important.* Say that *India matters.* Just say the words, and our poor, fragile, and insecure brown souls will be healed."

Without *your* validation, you see, we are nothing! It is hard not to see the comparison with the previous generations of black American writers, as described by Richard Wright: "entering the Court of American Public Opinion dressed in the knee-pants of servility, curtsying to show that the Negro was not inferior, that he was human, and that he had a life comparable to that of other people."

But why *shouldn't* we direct our energies towards impressing the whites? What is left for any of us in the physical India anyway? Some Indians respond, not entirely without justification. India has no charismatic leaders, no more Gandhis, no striptease shows, no *Moulin Rouge*, no rivers of Scotch, no bacchanalian revelries, nothing more than a few pathetic and painful metropolitan shows called cabarets. If there are any pygmy-statured Indian leaders left, those who haven't already made impressing the whites their life's agenda, which of them are *we* going to impress? And what would be the point? We would only be miserable and poor, forced to bear the company of other low-class Indians, the long-distance spitters, the comic-accented buffoons, the crooked-nosed freaks of Salman Rushdie's India, and the newly emerging and intolerable Hindu fanatics. We'd still have to go to Them (the whites) to get visas, and since all of us urban upper-middle-class Indians have citizens or greencard-holders of Western countries in the family, or lust after greencard-holding in-laws and foreign-student visas for our children, they have us by the short and curlies.

So all of us — I included — have a secret agenda in impressing the whites: the prospects of golden sex, megabucks, Bofors-sized[6]

---

[6] The notorious scandal has it that Bofors, the Swedish gun-manufacturer, gave tens of millions of dollars in kickbacks to a highly placed Indian political family in exchange for a massive contract for the supply of guns.

kickbacks, sparklingly clean swimming pools and spas, large stretches of empty beaches, mammoth libraries that actually lend you *audiotapes* and *videotapes*, massage parlors in which luscious women guiltlessly and 100 percent legally knead you in the nude, with no cop threatening to burst in and hijack forever your name, your fame, and your *sharam* or shame.

Even our gurus make it big, I mean maha-big, only when they impress the whites. (Give me a guru who has not a single Western disciple, and I'll give you a guru who is secretly practicing his English diction: *How now brown holy cow?*) So much so that it is easier to be admitted into some of India's own upscale ashrams if you are white-skinned; you have more privileges, they're not scowling at you or keeping a wary eye on you to grab you the moment you stray away from the official areas or try to decamp with their precious plastic spoons.

The problem is partly caused by the shamefully huge disparity in economic resources between the West and the Third World. The West is a Jupiter-sized cow with a billion bursting teats, and the rest of the world is five billion mouths fighting to suckle a drop from one emaciated cow (with two working teats, the third being on a labor strike, and the fourth awaiting an Ayurvedic massage to unclog its overworked ducts. Therefore, milking the West has become a major Third World industry, art, or con game — one that we must master merely to survive. We are practiced milkers, and we'll do almost anything, say almost anything, act any degrading role that's called for — all for a drop of the gleaming, life-giving, white stuff.

Some of us look out for missionary milk, others thirst for foreign conference milk, and millions more for job milk or Green Card milk. Decadents and sensualists yearn for tourist, Scotch, and red light district milk, academics connive to suckle *phoren* Ph.D. fellowship milk or Visiting Professor milk, while Eastern feminists — a la Alice Walker of *The Color Purple* — paint their brown husbands and brothers as black monsters and milk the gratefully dripping Western feminist Monster Teats.[7] According to a highly placed medical friend,

---

[7] American blacks also have had to study this art. As James Baldwin writes in *Notes*

even a well-known missionary hospital in Southwestern India maintains a fictitious list of drug addicts so it can milk the Western Anti-Drug Fanatics' milk.

Last come the Indian writers writing in English — who, emaciated by the watered-down and adulterated milk drops served by their scandalously few and notoriously parsimonious Indian patrons, are looking for prime literary milk: whether the Suitable Boy Hampshire Cow variety or the Exotic Freak Jersey Cow variety (translation rights, lucrative prizes, zillion-dollar advances).

So general and complete is the spread of this cancer that even wealthy Third Worlders belonging to the ghee-fed milk-baby elite catch the bug and succumb to the general frenzy of milking the West, though they are more selective, looking for sweetheart deals, kickbacks, expensive gadgets, multiple citizenships or green cards, and exotic cheeses and single-malt Scotch whiskies (a taste that filters down to a not-so-wealthy top editor I know). The reason why India has no large community of professional anarchists, while having disproportionately large numbers of feminist theorists, Yeats scholars, E. M. Forster thesis-writers, or structuralists? Because, by definition, no anarchist milk may be suckled from the West; anarchists are too disorganized or anti-organization to know where their cows are, let alone to arrange for them to mate with their bulls and ship the calves to their Indian fellow travelers.

For all this frenzy and massive effort, however, not much of the West's overflowing milk actually reaches the common people of the Third World, after the middlemen have taken their share. Besides which, the West, being the West, would rather dump its surplus milk, butter, and cheese — literally, as well as figuratively — into the ocean than ship these to the hungry (it justifies this act with some abstruse economic theory that escapes my humanist logic). Common

---

of a Native Son, "It is *part of the price the Negro pays for his position in this society* that, as Richard Wright points out, he is almost always acting. A Negro learns to gauge precisely what reaction the alien person facing him desires, and he produces it with disarming artlessness." [italics mine]

Americans often grumble that America spends too much on foreign aid instead of helping its own people, when in fact American charity, despite being a measly fraction of its GNP, gives America more reliable returns than Internet stocks.

No wonder that, fifty years after independence — and I say this with a heavy heart, knowing that this discovery may hurt other gentle souls whom I love, just as it has hurt me — Indians are still a slave nation (as indeed are most non-white nations of the world, excepting Japan and a few other countries which escaped long colonization). We are slaves to the Inner White that has been enshrined in our hearts, even in the remote corners of India,[8] so much so that we, of our own accord, metaphorically resurrect the Crawling Order (a real order, imposed by British Brigadier General R.E.H. Dyer in a certain part of Amritsar, requiring all Indians to crawl on all fours on a certain stretch of a public road). If an African woman had married into the Nehru family, would she have ever stood a chance of almost becoming Prime Minister, as the Italian-born Sonia Gandhi almost did? We will remain a slave nation until we realize the folly of our willing subjugation to the White West and make it a subject of national and universal discussion, even if we have to miss a few episodes of *Larry King Live*. For it is as true of us in India, as it is true of the blacks in the West Indies, as it is of the middle class blacks of America, as it is even of the Gucci-wearing women of Japan: so long as we try to impress the Other — the white, superior Other — not only will we never succeed (because it will never be enough, for that last one percent of approval will always be withheld), but we will never be happy, and we will never ever be true to ourselves.

I say that we are slave to our Inner White, but I do not mean to imply that our condition *equals* slavery. Because I do not dream of comparing the phenomenon I am describing as being even a fraction as grim as the subhuman treatment of African and other slaves in history (nor is Comparative Suffering my specialty), nor do I wish to

---

[8] And in the remote corners of Mongolia and Manchuria, where, I am told, the mannequins in the store windows are . . . white!

trivialize the word or the institution. I also admit that the role I speak of can also enslave a few whites, who are imprisoned in their roles, all the while uncomfortable with power, privilege, and adulation (a discomfort I wouldn't mind bearing, for a change).

But it is no use trying to tell me or Puerto Ricans that colonialism is history, because "the last colony," Macau, has just been granted independence. Why shouldn't the whites physically depart from the colonies? For they can comfortably return home, secure in the knowledge that they have planted their colonies inside their former subjects' heads, where they are now indestructible. Why not let the natives rule themselves (or think they do)? Who needs the headaches? Who needs to look bad? (And how can you not help looking bad when you have, let's say, the water-supply and a million other problems of two billion people on your plate?).

The average Occidental now has far more cash and leisure; he doesn't need to spend years in some small, mosquito-ridden Indian town to acquire his Eastern experience. He can afford a vacation home in the Caribbean, and he has imported his servants from various parts of the East: a huge proportion of the West's busboys, housemaids, babysitters, nursing assistants, lawn-service personnel, latrine cleaners, and other menials are imported labor from the former colonies — including, now, economic colonies of the West such as Latin America and Southeast Asia, and other countries which are too impoverished to afford their citizens a job, let alone a decent wage. If you can be pampered in your own country, and in a few select, remarkably unspoiled and relatively unpeopled paradises like the Caribbean Islands, Mexico, Greece, and the Canary Islands, why bother going gray and batty living in some mosquito-bitten, flea-ridden, disease-overrun *real* Third World country and racking your brains trying to solve their intractable problems? Or if you do, like the Americans and Britons who go in for fabulously salaried jobs in Arab countries, you can be sure that your skin color is doing 80 percent of the work for you and earning 80 percent of your salary, and you can treat your superprofits as "hardship" pay for having to look (and smile) at those towelheads and those corny camel sculptures day after day after day.

As the British say, "The King is dead; long live the King."

So it is with colonialism — which we all thought of as ended, but which, not having to operate as blatantly as it did according to the old rules, has reappeared in a new and more intractable form with the added requirement that those who would perform on an international stage, and even, often, those who must impress their own countrymen, are still required to impress the whites.

Think of this requirement as an absence of freedom: the absence of the freedom to be who one truly is. Think of it as a servile, inauthentic, and demeaning behavior forced on one because of one's ethnic group's perceived lack of influence in world affairs. Think of it as the New International Slavery.

DADDY, AM I A BLACK?

[An Almost-Impressing-the-Whites Essay]

Did you think, when you removed the gags from their mouths, that they would chant your praise?
— Jean Paul Sartre, *Black Orpheus*

One day, my five-year-old son came home from kindergarten with a look of concern on his face. "Daddy, the other children in my class said to me today that I am a black. I told them, 'No. My grandmother is black, but I am white.' Daddy, am I a black?"

James, like my two other sons, is an American citizen, and the son of Indian parents — parents from the real sub-continent of India, ten thousand miles away on the other, darker side of the planet. From his Indian parents, he has inherited a love for dosas, tandoori chicken, and boiled rice mixed with white, plain yogurt.

James is also, despite his light brown skin, one of the most splendid and seductive Americans I have known: an innocent, a helper, a sharer, unquenchably enthusiastic for knowledge and life, one who had gone through two years of pre-school being universally loved by his classmates and never for a moment considering himself different. Obviously, the kindergartners in his nearly all-white school in this middle-class Long Island neighborhood had now become aware of a color scheme dividing God's children, a two-tone color scheme in which you were either black or white.

My first impulse was to react the way most Indians do, the way I myself have responded once or twice, unthinkingly and perhaps with cowardice, to a misinterpretation of my skin color: "We are not black, we are not white. We are Indians."

But the involvement of my child now endowed the question with a wicked complexity, making me hate the question itself, bringing forth memories, making me want to tell him the truth of my experience . . . that color causes pain. That color causes condescension. That color causes invisibility. That, even though I knew many racist Indians and many exceptionally anti-racist Americans, it didn't make me feel any better whenever a white American, to whom I had been introduced on a previous social occasion, obliterated my existence with a blank look of non-recognition ("All you coloreds look the same"?). Or that once, at a convention of the American Society of Journalists and Authors, I was told firmly by a literary agent that I would be unlikely to be able to write English the way an American did.

But James was just an innocent child, gloriously free of my prejudices — and America had been good to him. In five years of life, he had run through more than a hundred toys, whereas in the first twenty years of life, his father had about five, mostly cheap thingamajigs that lasted around three days. He had a chance to get a wonderful education, free. And he was that sacred, awesome thing, the unattainable dream of many unfortunate millions around the world: an American citizen entitled to a crack at the American way of life. And for whom many an American President was and is willing to rush spunky troops and smart bombs halfway across the world.

So it would be unkind to contaminate his rosy innocence with my agonized, passionate feelings about the color standard. And if I couldn't corrupt him with my experience, could I at least give him an upbeat philosophical lecture on blackness, on how color is neutral, on how it has no moral value ... that color is a state of mind, and just part of God's scheme for human diversity?

I couldn't, not only because some of that was bullshit, but because he wanted a concrete answer. And wasn't this, after all, a matter-of-fact question about color?

But the precise color of my skin is rather imprecise. I am often mistaken for Arab, Latin American, or Iranian ("Go back to Eye-ran! A — hole!" passing motorists had sometimes yelled at me during the

Iranian hostage crisis in the last year of the Carter presidency). After many months without exposure to the sun, as at the end of a vacationless winter, I may even be asked — admittedly by the not-too-perceptive — if I am Greek or Italian or Turkish. Which goes to show that color in itself doesn't tell too many tales. Despite its ghastly importance in human affairs, skin color is pretty unreliable as a teller of stories. Still, your color had better not tell the wrong tale.

But it often does. In a world where whites are never snow-white, "yellows" are often "whiter" than so-called whites, and some "blacks" are more white than black, my color is a kind of wheat tone; which, in the white parts of the world, is a kind of invisible.

But I knew this answer wouldn't satisfy my son; it wouldn't satisfy his friends.

And actually, though it was . . . it wasn't really a question about color. It wasn't a question about him as much as it was a question about me, about the Indian-American identity, about the place of colored people in American society.

But what was wrong with saying, "I'm not black. I'm Indian?" I was reminded of a story related to me by an American pen pal in 1968, when I was still in school. It was about a snubbed and shunned dark-skinned Indian living in a Mississippi town. When the locals finally discovered his (Asian) Indian origins, they said, "But why didn't you *say* so?"

He replied, with Gandhian integrity, "I make no apologies for my color."

It's true that Indians in America, often coming from relatively privileged upper-middle-class backgrounds in their own country, are often better-educated, have more doctors, engineers, and scientists per capita among them than many other ethnic groups, not excluding whites. But it was precisely because of this that an answer such as "I'm not black. I'm Indian" was a betrayal of the brotherhood of the Invisible. Because such an answer really seemed to say, with pathetic black-and-white thinking: "Please, White Man or White Woman, treat me right. Because, you see, *we're not black, we're Indian*! I know, that can never mean quite as much to you as being German or Italian or even, dare I say it, Japanese, but please don't shun us quite as much as you do the blacks."

I wanted to avoid answering my son's question. I wanted to tell him: Color is only skin deep. I wanted to say: You're not black, you're not white, you're just beautiful. I wanted to say: You're not black, you're not white, you are a human being.

None of this would work with the gang, with his peer group, with his in-crowd, which was about to make him an outsider.

Besides, to say that color doesn't matter . . . What a black lie (which, as we all know, is worse than a white lie!) The language we all speak, the language that it is now virtually decreed the civilized world will speak forever (or until it blows itself up), the language that I love most — the language of Shakespeare and Pynchon and Ishmael Reed — also happens to be a language in which white is the color of virtue and of Snow White, black the color of evil, of dirt, of beastliness, of black magic and devilry. The preference for white, the hatred of black, is as ingrained in the language as melanin in a Nigerian's skin. Blackguard, black thoughts (Hamlet), black mark, blackmail, black sheep, pot calling the kettle black . . . with the possible and tasty exception of Blackened Cajun Chicken . . . .

But was I not blowing the matter out of proportion? Wasn't it within bounds for the Indian to state his Indianness up front? Isn't it natural for Indians, hailing mostly from their country's better-off classes and coming to America for a *better* life (unlike the Vietnamese boat people, who came for *life* itself), being quite high up in the American social order (with some downward adjustments for their skin color, of course), to not want to be identified with their new country's most oppressed class — however unjust the latter's oppression?

No doubt we Indians, marked by our appearance in the country of immigrants' dreams, crave for an identity, especially when faced with Columbus's long-forgiven and socially sanctified goof, by which "Indian" now refers to the so-called American Indian (though the politically correct language is Native American, most people continue to use the word "Indian"). We crave to be understood and appreciated for who we are. It dismays us — we, who know so much about America and other parts of the world — that we are so peripheral to the American consciousness, that the average American knows so little about India. That India, with one-seventh of the world's population (and with Indian immigrants forming about 1/200th of the present American population) comprises a far smaller fraction of the characters shown on American television and movie screens than, say, alien monsters or Ninja turtles. In other words, as far as Hollywood and the television networks go, the only good (Asian) Indian is a dead — or invisible — Indian.

"It's not a racist thing," an Indian friend had said, defending the tendency of Indians to view themselves as not black, but Indian. "We just don't want to be an anonymous thing called black. It's a human thing, wanting an identity. The blacks have their identity, we have ours. And we are proud of our identity, just as they are proud of theirs."

A fair-skinned Indian friend of mine had gone even further, claiming that according to him, he indeed was white: He always listed himself, in Census and Personnel office forms, as a Caucasian — explaining that his ancestors were the Aryans who came over to India from Central Europe, five thousand years ago, and that our tan had become somewhat permanent because our history was the equivalent of ten thousand continuous vacations in the Bahamas. "We are brown," said another Indian, holding up his hand for me to see, "Can't you see that?"

Maybe he was, but there were 900 million other Indians spanning a rainbow spectrum of hues. What about them? This may make many color-conscious Indians cringe, but I say the choice of black ought to be a political choice, reminding us that we were once classed as blacks by the British and in South Africa's apartheid lexicon, and will probably continue to be wherever white power is threatened. So long as we shirked evaded blackness, even by complex fudging about race and precise color, we could be accomplices in a scheme that was a blot on humanity. Despite its temporary inconveniences, I thought self-righteously, black was the right color to be.

35

And so, though a part of me wanted to protect my son's few glorious years of innocence, perhaps with some charming magical story that I might make up about some mischievous angel at Creation in a Holi frame of mind merrily spraying different colors on different people as we do during India's festival of Holi, I said to him, "So what if you are a black? There is nothing wrong with being a black."

He considered my statement for a moment. Then he said, slowly but firmly, "Daddy, I am *not* a black." To my surprise, I smiled at his politically incorrect choice and decided, out of regard for his greenness, to back off for now — and only for now — from the question of color. Perhaps, in a deeply philosophical sense, he was not completely wrong. True, in America, at least in the next few, formative decades, his color will always be second best, never the right one. But perhaps, in the multi-colored America of the future, it would matter a little less than it does now.

* * *

If this is an unsatisfactory ending to my tale, it may be that there can be no neat conclusion to this constantly evolving story. Except to say that two years later, my son had earned the respect of his second-grade classmates as the one who wrote the best, longest, and funniest stories among them, the one who read like a fourth-grader, the one who had an answer for everything, even subjects he knew nothing about. And that now, a few years later still, his younger brother is the darling of his first grade class.

It also happened, a short while ago, that I was taking a walk in the small New Hampshire town of Contoocook when two children, from the window of their roadside house, mocked me and shouted racial epithets at me. I was about to walk away, shushing the primal reaction of fury raging within me. They were only children, after all, and why should mere words, thoughtless words, exert such power over me? Then I decided the children needed to be corrected, or at least challenged, simply to protect the next, perhaps more-sensitive victim. I rang the bell and said I wanted to speak to their mother.

When their mother heard my story, she burst into tears and

apologized profusely, saying, "We aren't that kind of people. We have always taught them to respect other people." And I was moved: by her obvious sincerity, by the depth of her feelings. Had I been a black man living in the early part of this century — perhaps even a black man, living in some other parts of the America today, such as rural Mississippi — I could not have dreamt of getting such an apology. I left with a skip in my walk — an overreaction, no doubt, but it had been so long that an American had even *pretended* to apologize to me for a racial slight.

In a related incident, I had shown a draft of this essay to two retired Jewish neighbors, Faye and Dave, who seemed to practice the precept "Love Thy Neighbor" more than most Christians I know. My son James could, and would walk into their house at any time he pleased. He was like a grandson to them.

"Who did it?" Dave exploded, his face coloring as he read the part about my son's classmates having called him a black. "I'm going to beat them up." It was the primal instinct of someone who was going to protect his family from external danger.

Another overreaction, perhaps, but I was touched. In small changes like this, I have tried to look for hope, despite the continuing oppression of blacks, and despite the fact that policemen in my mainly white town still sometimes slow down when they see me walking alone to give me a long, close look — an invisible, creepy, shriveling look like a clammy, cold, subhuman hand on the back of my neck. Yes, I hope, because I must, that slowly, things will change. And at least in some cases, for the better.

* * *

"At least in some cases, for the better." Those were the optimistic words which ended the essay which I submitted to various publications including *The New York Times* and *Newsweek,* from around 1990 to 1994. And now for some post-essay analysis. What I now notice, looking back at my essay, is my *unconscious* attempt to tone down the passion of the beginning and the middle and, thus, with my goodness and nobility (and lack of bitterness or Third World entitlement, the hopeful sentiment about the "multi-colored America of the future", the appended anecdotes about nice white people), to "impress" the white editors of the *New York Times Magazine* or *Newsweek.*

That didn't happen, and believing the essay to be too good to submit to a limited-circulation newspaper, where it probably would have been published and forgotten, I kept it in my drawer, editing and expanding it in 1994, in perhaps a renewed *unconscious* attempt to make it sound upbeat enough as to impress white editors (Notice the "so what if he's brown? He's bright and successful" element added on to the piece? Along with the "there are really some decent white people, you know?" tidbit? For let's face it, as the *Village Voice* pointed out in a feature in 1995 or 1996, it's a white white white world out there in the magazine and publishing Olympuses of America, and let's not even talk about Sonny Mehta). It was as if I was trying to tell these white Makers of Our Destiny, "See what a cool guy I really am? Can you not love me *now*, at last?" And perhaps as an unconscious result of my visualization of these magazines, and my hopes of enticing their editorial *readers* (some twenty- one-year-old Ivy League graduate perhaps, since without a referral, the piece would never reach a senior editor?), the content and the feeling of it got watered down — because, and that's the lesson I had distilled from my experience at the time and the behavior of my more successful countrymen in America — our very existence in this Promised Land, this America, is conditioned on watering down our essence, our sadly prickly essence, almost down to one vast, undifferentiated American Goo with a slightly different flavor or color (FDA approved additive) for each ethnic group. The flavors, or Approved Flavors, being served by the respective brown house niggers who write for the Opinion pages of the top newspapers, who touch your white bleeding hearts, because despite all their suffering, they have . . . such good *attitude*!

The essay that follows was written a few years later, when I had abandoned even the slightest *unconscious* hope of, or desire for, "impressing the whites." In other words, I was beginning to get closer to writing what I felt to be the truth — despite having a hunch that my unvarnished truth might give many white, brown, yellow, black, and mixed color people the blues, and muddy my reputation.

THE FOURTEEN COMMANDMENTS OF INDIAN AND NONWHITE MALE SUCCESS

After fifteen years of prayer, meditation, observation, consultation, travel, experience, and little love offerings to the Goddess, combined with too little beer, no Ecstasy, and no pot whatsoever (I really *didn't* inhale), I had reluctantly come to the conclusion that to be accepted and successful in the white world, nonwhite men needed to obey the *Seven* Laws of Nonwhite Male Success in the Western World. (Please, it has been emphasized elsewhere in the book: the laws/rules for nonwhite women and nonwhite men are sometimes quite different.) Whereupon one night, in a dream, accompanied by thunder and lightning, a White God appeared before me and expanded my understanding manifold.

Reclining stylishly and self-consciously on a white cloud, smoking a cigar and wearing Gandhi-frame glasses, but otherwise looking very much like God in Michelangelo's rendering on the ceiling of the Sistine Chapel, the White God balanced a minutely inscribed coconut in each hand and roared in a deep-throated voice:

We are the White Gods, your Lords for the next trillion centuries of the New World Order. To get along lollygaggingly with us, to prosper in our New World Order, and to impress us mightily, thou shalt follow the Fifteen Commandments of Indian and Nonwhite (Male) Success — or the Coconut Bible. Well, as many of the following Fifteen Commandments as may apply to thee, but a minimum of seven in any case.

"Whassat?" I asked in a Ray Charles accent. I was dreaming, after all, and was allowed occasional comic liberties.

"Shaddup!" said the White God, "and write!

The First Commandment: Thou shalt not have any other-colored gods before us."

"None? Not even our own? Not even the Japanese?"
"What's the matter with you? Don't you understand English?"
"Yes, Massa! One mulligatawny soup coming right up, Massa!"

"The Second Commandment: Thou shalt be gurus, godmen, and charlatans."

Learned Commentary (in a second dream, a commentary came to me from a Pompous Pure Brahmin Professor Angel explaining repeatedly for my benefit): Give them a good show, a good circus, so that when the loot is finally tallied, there's enough of a cut for everyone involved, white, brown, and black.

"The Third Commandment: Thou shalt shave off your moustaches and your identities, and put distance between yourselves and things Indian."

Learned Brahmin Commentary: Going to Oxford or Cambridge and peppering your conversation with "I say, old chap!" or "Pass the roast beef, what ho!" might be passé, but it helps, partly because the certified British accent still makes American women wet their knickers. As for shaving off your moustaches or beards, it tends to make you look more effeminate and less threateningly exotic. Ok. That's always a help, particularly if you are otherwise imposing (reposing is okay). Colin Powell would certainly have stood not one chance in a zillion of becoming Chairman of the Joint Chiefs of Staff had he sported a devilish goatee, let alone a mullah's foot-long bush. A Bush in the White House is fine; a bush on a French artist's chin is

42

also somehow tolerable; but a bush on a brown man's face automatically gets him sent to the doghouse, or to a secret underground CIA prison, whichever is more convenient. Equally true for metaphysical bush.

"The Fourth Commandment: Thou shalt be unthreateningly short."

Commentary: How many tall, successful, West-approved, non-entrepreneurial Indians do you know? There's an easy psychological and historical explanation for why the Master Race prefers longitudinally disadvantaged persons among its brown boys. Many of its bad brown boys have been tall (Saddam, Gaddafi, and recently, Osama), whereas Indians or Asians of diminished stature, especially if they have large, Koala-bear eyes and look fragile, can easily be transformed in the Western preconscious or unconscious from threats to pets, from beasts to cuties (did I hear someone say 1-800-Hindoo-Teddy?). A diminished physical stature makes Western people more comfortable with you, because they know they are always in control, that any minute you present a threat, they could send you whimpering out the door like a poodle that has peed on its master's priceless Persian rug. Not only does this mean that Indians, being on the whole short and unthreatening, are permitted to buy houses in white neighborhoods that are closed to the tall and muscular descendants of the slaves who built America, but the list of short, wildly successful Indians is a mile long: Arundhati Roy, Vikram Seth, Jawaharlal Nehru, Sonny Mehta. Whereas the list of tall successful Indians, or even Asians, is an inch short; only Michael Ondaatje comes to mind, and he with his partial Dutch ancestry is so fair-skinned, he can almost pass off as white. And could that partly be the reason why Bali, the Philippines, and Thailand, whose residents are shorter than most North Indians, draw huge Western tourist arrivals in proportion to their respective populations?

What if you can't be a literary Bambi because Nature made you too tall or gave you a rough and uncuddly exterior? You might try carrying around your own teddy bear, shedding tears frequently (tears of gratitude are especially welcome), or learning to walk on your knees (which should trigger the sympathy response reserved for the handicapped). If that doesn't work, try surgery to shorten your legs — it will more than pay off. According to my formula, for every extra inch, penile or otherwise, deduct $100,000 from your potential book advance. For that final but desperately crucial inch, deduct half a million.

"The Fifth Commandment saith: Whether or not thou art longitudinally disadvantaged, in totality or in a specific portion of thy anatomy, thou shalt not forget to cultivate a completely asexual appearance and demeanor. The short version of this commandment is: Brown Boy? Down, Boy!"

Commentary: For example, never admit in your speech, writing, or emails to having sexual desires, let alone comment on sex loudly — especially within the hearing of a white woman. (See what ultimately happened to Osho Rajneesh, who was booted out of the United States, a well-known retirement haven for former contra thugs and dictators like the late Ferdinand Marcos, while sexually conservative Indian gurus quietly build empires? And see what happened to publishing superstar David Davidar, who had made all the right moves up until that point, except perhaps for being too tall — another decisive failing?) Be *subdued* in your masculine qualities (if you are a man, that is). Pretend you are far more interested in making money or in spiritual and artistic pursuits than you are in sex. Even better, preach sexual continence, purity, spirituality, and sublimation. (If you're a woman, of course, a little flirtatious cuteness or bedroom eyes cannot hurt — they might even be an asset.) Eunuchs are cute, after all, and accident-free. And as for money, the Masters appreciate it too, so long as there's a cut in it for them.

"Number Six Commandment saying: Don't be ethnic, except when following the Seventh or Twelfth Commandments."

Commentary: "Don't be ethnic," recommended a group of New York Indians seriously and solemnly discussing how best to impress Westerners. Meaning: talk, dress, behave, and think so much like "them" that, after all you have done to erase your ethnic origins, they simply cannot blame you for the unfortunate accident of your birth. Wear silk shirts and bowler hats, smoke pipes, know your Scotch, dress like a penguin (or better still, carry one around, a Penguin book if not the real thing), and get yourself noticed at the Royal Symphony. If you speak in English, acquire an accent more British than the Queen's. If you write English, write in a style that is more British than the British (this was how Amitav Ghosh impressed Anthony Burgess, how Nirad Chaudhuri impressed other Britons, and how Indrani Aikath Gyaltsen got some pretty big British and American backers until they found out she had plagiarized two English novels).

A corollary of this commandment is one I shall call Richard's Law of Melanin Content. A taxi-driver, a tourist guide, a writer: have you noticed that the lower the melanin content of the company any one of these keeps, the more successful he is? Salman Rushdie has really, really arrived (I mean, he is a sneeze away from the Nobel Prize), and colored people constitute hardly ten percent of his daily contacts (at least before he met his exotic young Indian model friend). A tourist guide having regular white clients is in big-money territory. There are taxi-drivers in Bombay who laze all day in their taxis, rejecting their brown customers, waiting for the one white customer who can make their day, or perhaps their week. Therefore, make a list of all the brown people in your life, starting with your spouse. Then lose them, and substitute them with white ones.

Turning his attention to the coconut in his right hand, the White God read:

"Commandment Number Seven: *Thou shalt be exotic.*"

Commentary: Does this not contradict the Sixth Commandment? Perhaps, but the compassionate White God wanted to give us poor wretched coloreds a choice. Yes, you can get away with flouting the Sixth if you cross over to the other extreme and play the exotic animal — strut your authenticity to the high heavens, write rip-roaring biriyani fiction, walk about Piccadilly with a penis ornament dangling from your exposed member, insisting that it happens to be an essential element of your cultural heritage. It also helps if you are an exotic woman who can feed the "sensitive" Westerners' hunger for instant cultural education with a lot of flirtatious yakkity-yak; a certain upper-class Bengali woman who studied at Columbia University a couple of decades back, before Indians became commonplace, proudly claims that she was fawned over for being exotic.

"Eighth Commandment (also known as the Son of Sonny Commandment): Subscribe to the New York City Opera and change your names to easily pronounceable, pettable ones such as Sweety, Pinky, or Bambi. Unless you already have a two-syllable, easily pronounceable Eastern name: Vi-kram, Sal-man, Dee-pack, A-shock."

Commentary: If you are an Easterner with a "Western" name, it embarrasses Westerners; your "Western" name reminds them of their shameful history of proselytization and of converting Easterners to religious ideas they themselves — the self-declared intelligent, liberal ones — have abandoned as laughably quaint and ridiculous. Christianized and de-exoticized Suzanna Arundhati Roy (her original name) will not do; it has to be Arundhati Roy. Even Allan Sealy (the Indian author happens to be Anglo-Indian, meaning he's had at least one English ancestor), despite his name's conformity to the two-syllable rule, doesn't ring "authentic", and therefore cannot rank as high on the scale of Orientalism (a la Edward Said) as Krishna Kant or Laloo Prasad Mithaiwalla. Whereas if you have a mouthable Eastern name, they love to "adopt" you, for it gets them 'brownie points' (no pun intended) for being broad-minded and racially tolerant and for being hospitable towards ethnic diversity.

This two-syllable rule does not apply to Indian women, who are allowed to have long and exotic names under the Oriental "Scheherazade" exception.

"Ninth Commandment: As a Beatles song advises, "Behave yourself!"

Commentary: I mean, really, *really* behave! If you are an Indian or an Easterner, the following attributes will make a terrifically favorable impression: nonviolence, spirituality, restrained and mild language, always saying you are sorry, purity, chastity, otherworldliness, hard work, an unquestioning nature, non-aggressiveness, vegetarianism, a habit of bending, bowing, yielding, and crawling before white people, and boundless hospitality (willingly meeting the needs of your light-skinned visitors, whatever these needs might be — and no, no need to be nice to African or other Third World visitors).

Never mind that some of the West's own popular figures, some with heroic or mythic stature, were violent, brash, foul-mouthed, sexually voracious, earthy, gobblers of red meat: Robert Clive (the British bad boy turned English conqueror), Lord Byron, John Kennedy (who was nicknamed Mattress Jack and had a Secret Service detail working overtime to smuggle him his blonde of the afternoon), Napoleon, Charlie Chaplin, Hemingway, Hunter Thompson, Madonna, Indian-roasting Christopher Columbus, and of course Mick "Throbbing Dick" Jagger, who supposedly sprinkled his personal holy water on to the sacred portals of over eighteen thousand women.

When a Westerner looks at a live Easterner, he *expects* meekness, mildness, spirituality, low sperm count, short invisible dicks, and inexhaustible patience. He will be most, most disappointed, and will punish you for the bad, bad boy you have been — lower your shorts, six of the best — if you do not reproduce the stereotype. Thou shalt behave and obey not jus the whites, but also their lackeys, assigns, cronies, agents, viceroys. Behave, don't complain, don't kick any dust, and you are rewarded. One day, you tell yourself, when you are powerful enough and don't need them anymore, you will speak up, you will be yourself, you will fight back. But when that day comes, it is already far too late, for you've lost your soul. A lifetime of behaving has made you into a real lackey, a real slave.

Of course, there's no prohibition against brown bad girls, or else I would mention Mae "Come Up and See Me Some Time" West and Marilyn Monroe, of whom someone said, "Copulation was Marilyn's uncomplicated way of saying Thank You." Indeed, naughty brown or yellow girls who are sexually suggestive and seductive and eager to please will attract premium prices and occasional 21-gun salutes of the This-is-my-rifle-this-is-my-gun variety. The prohibition against bad brown boys is absolute, though. Sorry, boys, we didn't say life was fair, did we? It may not make sense, it may not be true to human nature, and it may not suit you one day as you wake up on the wrong side of the bed and feel like yelling out a curse, but *don't do it! You are Eastern!* Like it or not, Eastern has become synonymous with spiritual in the minds of millions of Westerners (not a few of them consumers of New Age products and philosophies), and you simply cannot afford to upset the apple cart; besides, "bad brown boy" has become synonymous in the subconscious of many media-manipulated Westerners with "terrorist" and "Saddam Hussein." Therefore, that option is suicide.

What have Arundhati and Vikram Seth wrought? Following their much publicized examples, possibly ten thousand Indian writers, the cream of the cream, have decided to "behave", some thinking they would wait until they became rich to truly speak what they think; but after years of this, they wake up, one day (or never wake up), to discover that it is too late: they have lost their soul. For the West to have thus controlled India's best minds with what is small change for them, is a coup bigger than the stealing of the Kohinoor Diamond; while they do this, our Indian billionaires hang on tightly to their ill-gotten potlis or moneybags, or build temples and garish palaces with them — not understanding that a few independent minds, minds that have credibility because they have been independent from Day 1, and simply cannot be bought — could be their most precious investment.

Perhaps, at the end of all this writing and fighting, I have not much to be proud of, but this much I can say, with Frank Sinatra-ish pride: *I misbehaved from the very first*, from the very first line of the very first page of my very first book (*The Revised Kama Sutra*, read the original Viking Penguin hardcover or the Invisible Man Books edition). And I wrote most of it *my way*. [End of Brahmin Commentary.]

"Tenth Commandment: Thou shalt kiss white ass."

"Please, God," said, I. "Can you not be a little more subtle?"

"I am God," said God. "I don't have to be subtle. Subtlety is for slaves, wimps, and con men."

Commentary: So estimable are we Indians in this department, so much is flattery and soft-soaping a part of our culture — especially of North Indian culture — that even the best among us unconsciously slip into a mild form of it at times, suddenly losing the friendship or potential friendship of Westerners who are allergic to the practice. How then can flattery be a recipe for success in the West if it also turns off Westerners? Because the ass-kissing of successful Indians is as subtle and sophisticated as imitation. Imitating *their* manners, *their* dress, and *their* very thoughts, hailing as we do from a sophisticated culture, is extremely compelling and effective, because by doing so we proclaim that their style of life is the Ultimate, the Apogee of Human Civilization. But crude fawning will not work; it is quite likely to boomerang.

"Eleventh Commandment: Thou shalt monkey around for our amusement and pleasure."

Commentary: A few monkey tricks in your arsenal are money in the bank. Western people don't just love cute little dogs; their hearts also go out to vulnerable monkeys, who — along with their relatives from the San Diego Zoo — have received more coverage on 20 years of the *Tonight Show with Johnny Carson* than 900 million Indians combined. Why? Because when you monkey around, they suddenly remember that you, brown simian that you are, are related to them by blood, by your common membership in the family of Primates. Monkeying around with their language gets you good marks if you are a writer.

The more bizarre the costume and your behavior (so long as it is non-threatening and can pass as "culture" or "tradition"), the more you will please the Masters. For example, at a Festival of India in the Mall in Washington D.C., the largest crowd was gathered around a bizarrely dressed family that was dancing, climbing a pole, whacking a drum, and so on, engaging in some traditional monkey business. It is my guess that the moment the male member of the group returned to India, he flung off his ridiculous costume, wriggled into his foreign-purchased Calvin Klein jeans and Hong Kong imitation Rolex watch, and dashed off to the nearest McDonald's to munch on the goat-flavored bliss of a pure mutton Big Mac while he condescendingly looked down his nose and through the glass window at the bloody "natives."

"Twelfth Commandment: Thou shalt be a game-player: that is, thou shalt gamely cooperate with the games we play on you: for example, Divide and Conquer."

Commentary: Play along as we Divide and Conquer your races, your sexes, your social classes, your shades of skin color. Also, thou shalt capture and turn in to our custody any among you who, proven guilty or not, is wanted by us for questioning, torture, disablement, or extinction. When you do that, we shall be tremendously impressed by how nonracist and selfless and democratic and pro-freedom you are.

The archetype of this commandment was created by the pair of Robert Clive (the British East India Company general) and Mir Jaffar in the eighteenth century. Mir Jaffar was an Indian general who betrayed his boss, the Nawab of Bengal, by facilitating an English military victory that gave England effective control over Bengal in return for his promotion to nominal rulership of that province. Perhaps the truer original model for this kind of betrayal was Judas

Iscariot, who betrayed Jesus for a paltry thirty pieces of silver — indeed, Judas may even have had a little Indian blood in him — since many Indians will undercut each other to do the Masters' dirty work for twenty pieces of silver, or maybe even ten, five, two, or for nothing at all, just to serve You, the Masters, and to prove what loyal doggies they are! Woof woof! Me, me, me!

Thirteenth (Optional) Commandment: Thou shalt choose thy parents wisely. (Valid for fifteen brownie points; 50 brownie points earn you a knighthood from the Queen.)

Commentary: While it is true in almost any culture that getting yourself a powerful or rich or influential or talented father or mother (or in the absence of either, a godmother/godfather) is a smart move for getting ahead in life — especially in politics or business — an examination of Indian writers who have been successful in the West reveals that a startling 80 to 90 percent of these have chosen their parents wisely, compared with famous American writers, who are, most of the time, not born into special privilege. (Imagine an American literature in which the only writers in the canon were graduates of Harvard, Yale, Princeton, and Cornell? It would be a poor literature indeed!) Among Indian writers there is of course Rushdie, who chose a millionaire father who sent him to Eton and Cambridge. Then there is Vikram Seth, whose mother is a High Court Judge. Amitav Ghosh, Nayantara Sahgal . . . the list goes on and on. With the help of well-connected parents such as these, you can become a player in the British class system by getting into a good Indian or Western public school and finally going on to Cambridge or Oxford University, and if not, at least to the Ivy League universities — after which, your life is pretty much made.

Fourteenth (Optional) Commandment: If thou be a babe, thou shalt be gorgeous and photogenic and food for our fantasies (a few exceptions made for gushingly grateful, not completely dead babes, especially in America, which gets orgasms from listening to immigrants expressing their gratitude). If thou art a boy, thou shalt be effeminate and suitable.

Commentary: Rushdie is an exception to the above commandment, but then, he is almost one of Them, and he has the demeanor and arrogance of a Grand Mughal, or a Suleiman the Magnificent; the rules don't apply to him. Also, once you've won a Nobel, your skin color doesn't matter. Rules are only for mortals, and with a Nobel (or a double Booker), you are no longer a mortal; you're a god.

* * *

Of course, these Commandments may not work for everyone. You may be handicapped by a rebellious spirit, a genetic program possibly, which makes it impossible for you to accept a neutered and circumscribed literary existence. Or you may have literary heroes — Kamala Das, Henry Miller, Kurt Vonnegut, and Richard Wright — who never compromised, and you will not, either

What about those who do not run into such genetic obstacles? Should all nonwhites follow these Commandments, since the supremacy of the Western world is guaranteed for at least a few hundred more years, if not a thousand — or until the Chinese develop a Superbomb? Not necessarily. It is a good thing that some of us — Mahatma Gandhi, for instance — are a little dim in the upper story, or slow learners. Had Gandhi understood and followed the Twelve/Fourteen/Fifteen Commandments of Indian Success in the West, he would most likely have ended his life as a wealthy South African lawyer with four Rolls Royces and the best-tailored clothes in Cape Town. Unless, of course, he emigrated to America, where he would have Americanized his name to Mac Gandson ("Little Mac" to his friends Billy Kumar and Sam Patel) or Moe Gand and become the most conscientious and *nonviolent* ambulance chaser and motel chain operator west of Greenland.

MONICA LEWINSKY'S THONG UNDERWEAR
Or, Black and White and Towards Oneness

What do Elizabeth Taylor's husbands, Princess Stephanie's escapades, Madonna's baby, some celebrity's diet or thighs, Cher's boob jobs, or Monica Lewinsky's thong underwear — all in the last few years the subject of vast acres of print space, speculation, and public comment in the Western media — have to do with the world's color schemes?

I'll come to that in a moment; meanwhile, my intent is to examine and challenge the vocabulary and fairness of the world's color bars, even if I sometimes use that terminology myself. For I do not believe in walls, divisions, and doors. I believe we should throw open the doors of the Harvard Club, the Princeton Club, the Groucho Club, and the immigration gates at New York and Heathrow to all who would enter. Let us stop demanding visas and documentary proof from the brown-skinned, while letting white people whiz through the customs checkpoints of life. This often literally happens at Canadian entry points bordering the United States — and sometimes even in Third World countries, where customs officials (like black police officers in America) often treat white people better than their fellow nationals or similarly colored non-nationals. And if we must have national borders for the sake of administrative convenience or history, then let the United Nations (or the United States, by whose grace and mostly unpaid dues the United Nations exists and functions as a debating society) see to it that every human being becomes a citizen of at least three countries partly by choice and partly by random lottery. Let at least one of these three countries be a developing country, and by this I mean one of the twenty largest and most problematic developing countries, not some banana republic or tropical paradise such as Belize. By enforcing universal multiple citizenship, we might dilute humankind's inherent chauvinistic tendencies.

But so long as this does not happen, and so long as we do in fact categorize, reward, punish, and exclude people based on their skin color, race, or national origin, a race-neutral public vocabulary would only hide the ugliness of reality, the truth of prejudice, and help it to prosper. Until universal multiple citizenship or open borders become a reality, let us call things by their true names. For to understand the lies and fictions and mislabelings that oppress us, to analyze the appropriateness of the labels used to define our limits, might be a first step towards the ultimate dropping of labels.

For example, to label Salman Rushdie and Vikram Seth "black British writers," as a London *Observer* piece did recently, is silly. The distinction that I am making is not about color, mind you; a startling range of skin colors flourish in India, but most Indians still share some common element called "Indianness," which is about something far deeper than color: a world-view, a history, a shared culture, certain cultural and personal habits such as excessive thrift and a certain introversion, inhibition (except in Punjab), individualism, and a greater emphasis on learning and mental achievement.

It is time to find a new method of describing people, a method other than the color of their skin — which is startlingly not black, for example, in the cases of authors Salman Rushdie and Ameena Meer, whose socially exalted births and fair and lovely skins make them nearly immune to racial prejudice in white company, or to the obliterating invisibility experienced by the middle-class small-town Indian. (Indeed, these two worthies, by their mere presence, give most middle-class *whites* an inferiority complex.) The current color standard, ordained by the white Powers-that-Be who dominate the Security Council with their votes — I mean, their vetoes — ensures that the huge four-fifths of the world falling under the general category of "black" or "nonwhite" must fight each other merely to be heard; and often their "chosen" representatives do not truly represent them, having successfully reinvented themselves as whites.

In the literary version of this Divide-and-Conquer game, the result is a squabble among the colored for the privilege of being the official, white-sanctioned spokespersons for their race. At the higher levels of the nonwhite world, people perform frantic dances, bows, toe-sucks, headstands, or whatever other monkey tricks it takes to prove that *they* are "real" Indians, Africans, or Papuans, while their peers are not. In the business of being appointed or anointed the official spokesperson for your race or ethnic group, there is a tidy fortune to be made. So it is important to recognize that being black, brown, yellow, or white today is not a matter of color so much as it is a matter of power and complicity.

In many Caribbean islands, there are *black* Governors General who function by Her White British Majesty's grace (how kind, how very kindhearted and thoughtful of Her) and at her strictly theoretical pleasure (one assumes she is too stiff to be capable of real pleasure). Similarly, ex-brown persons have been granted Honorary Whiteness — Oxbridge degrees, knighthoods, prestigious prizes, or other forms of Western recognition — which they use to preen themselves and keep a respectable and safe distance from their less fortunate former desiwallahs (or fellow countrymen).

But how can you truly represent brown people when you are cozier with your race's oppressors than with your own fellowmen, when you've whitened your brain and your insides to the extent that you are called a "coconut" (an unkind term, perhaps, but brilliantly self-explanatory)?

Boo to those who would use the term *race card* to try to intimidate you into keeping mum about racial discrimination—thus, in effect, allowing it to flourish with impunity. For the reality is that the race-card game is virtually the only card game in town. It is a game in which the white people hold all the aces and are the kings and queens, while blacks are the knaves of spades, the browns the knaves of hearts, and all the colored races take turns being the jokers.

There are those who would point to multi-racial but colored Tiger Woods and say, "Let's not talk about race anymore." I believe that people who hold this viewpoint, which I call Tiger Woodsism, do so quite sincerely. But, while the world is indeed getting much more diverse and racially mixed, a few score exceptions like Tiger Woods, Michael Jackson, or Michael Jordan do not mitigate the real obstructions faced by the vast majority who are not Silicon Valley millionaires or multi-racial successes. To the vast majority, racial oppression is still alive and well and constantly adapting itself to the times, and Tiger Woodsism (or Colin Powellism) works in effect as a tool of propaganda to muzzle and to continue to oppress the colored majority.

So what am I? Black, Brown, Indian, Asian? Am I not rather simply a human being who happens to be a satirist and an exile?

I despise and detest labels and divisiveness of any kind: Christian, New Age, vegan, Viking, tree hugger, lesbian ventriloquist — because all such labels diminish the complex human being they refer to, and make us forget that we are all, or should be one humanity. However, let us confine ourselves to the issue of race and nationality for the moment. In an ideal world, I would agree wholeheartedly with the intellectuals' guru, Jiddu Krishnamurthy, who says that "to say 'I am an Indian' is a violent act, because by it you separate yourself from the rest of humanity." But this "violence" is partly the result of the nearly universal *questions*, in visa application forms, at immigration checkpoints, in census forms, and in various social exchanges: *What is your nationality?* or *Are you an Indian?* Or even worse, *But you look Indian!* So long as these questions continue to be asked, often with an immediate penalty attached to the answers — so long as to be an Indian is, as Indian author Pico Iyer says of his experience in Japan, "the lowest of the low" (and he's an Oxford-educated, world-recognized author, with status, and married to a Japanese woman, not some coolie) — then to camouflage or hide your Indianness or your minority status is to run away from it, with only a temporary benefit to yourself, but much greater benefit to those who would put you down, who would intimidate you for having been born to the

"wrong" parents. In my own experience, I've often found that —
except in parts of California, where a certain awe attaches to the label
"Indian" — a conversation is often ended moments after I reveal my
nationality; in most consular visa offices, the revelation immediately
causes my documentary requirements and fees to quadruple.

Truly abolish all such questions and the discrimination that flows
from them, and I shall heartily endorse an experimental move to
abandon national and racial identity. To abandon the discussion of
national identity without the abolition of the attached penalties will
be to yield to a Global Disney Village in which the race-free
camaraderie or brotherly tolerance is illusory and faked and shallow
— a commercial fiction, a Disney-Coca Cola opiate to enable the
transnational corporations to sell, sell, and sell more.

In plain English: well-meaning white people need to understand
that the reason we colored people become conscious of our skin
color once we move to the West is that, almost every moment of our
lives, white society does not allow us to forget it.

In these circumstances, let us accept the impracticality of
Krishnamurthy's noble sentiments, and let us boldly proclaim who
we are. Let us at the same time declare the act of *discriminating* against
persons to be a real act of violence; the true act of violence is not
your saying "I am an Indian," but the visa officer's response, "You're
an *Indian*? Sorry, then. In that case, you'll have to spend a hundred
dollars and wait three months for a visa before you enter our
country." And until things improve, we from the invisible classes of
invisible countries must ferret out hidden injustices, question
impostors and coconuts, fight mental colonialism and the
phenomenon of New Invisible People, and work for a true diversity
of voices rather than a managed diversity.

And as for who or what I am, and what color? Until we can have a
world that doesn't need labels, *my color will be Third World*. And my
identity: *an exiled No-Man*.

There will still be those authorities of all sorts who will demand,
"Give me a color, quick, and don't waste my time. Black, white, or
yellow?"

And I will not voluntarily oblige. For I oppose the division of peoples into *primary* colors. This is too simplistic a categorization, one that becomes an easy excuse for the ignorance and indifference of the powerful, who are mostly rich and pale-skinned, towards the weak, who are mostly poor and coal-black (well, I was getting a bit colorful here—I mean, dark-skinned). I would rather that white people took the trouble to study and understand our true and complex identities, our backgrounds, our nuances.[9] Getting to know us is not easy, I admit, my esteemed white friends — but it is important that *you* do the work, that *you* have the humility to do it, and to understand its necessity, especially when You devote so much attention to such trivialities as Michael Jackson's nose job or Cher's new breasts. It is far more important to the fate of the Earth that You Westerners (who decide so much of its fate, and also where the bombs will fall) be better able to distinguish between Africans and Indians, or South Indians and North Indians, or Sikhs and Indian Christians, and less likely to label all Indians as cow-worshipers, book-burners, rioters, or Peter Sellers-like klutzes.

"Oh, but Americans don't even know their own Senators' names!" I'm often told. "Their ignorance has nothing to do with racism!"

"Sorry," I reply, "Ignorance is not an acceptable excuse. Ignorance is not benign when it comes to ethnic groups and cultures. Indeed, ignorance is itself a kind of prejudice, for in a society where knowledge is so abundantly available, willful ignorance communicates a choice and a value judgment — a judgment that Indians, West Indians, Africans, or other colored people are not important or worthwhile enough to know about, while dinosaurs, Pamela Anderson's breast implants, Madonna's lovers, and Monica's thong underwear are."

---

[9] Rather than, as Pratap Rughani observes in *New Internationalist Magazine*, to present or feed on "images of the South that process eighty percent of the world's population into a quick cliché." Deborah McLaren, who quotes Rughani in her extraordinary book, *Rethinking Tourism and Eco Travel*, laments tourist brochures that are "the opposite of famine pornography . . . [with] endless brown and black people smiling and saying, 'I want to be your friend.'"

I close with a story of Oneness, or of a moment of Oneness in my life. It is a moment all of us need to have more often. And I must tell it, even at the risk of seeming to want to impress the liberal white reader.

It is January 1999, and I am driving behind a car in Aventura, North Miami. I am crawling along on a three-lane road on which access to the other two lanes is impossible because of the densely packed traffic. So I am stuck behind this snail-like woman driver for another three minutes, until we both make a right turn into a lightly traveled two-lane road, and I overtake her and glare at her sideways, fuming and angry. She is a white woman, about seventy-five years old. All of a sudden, I say to myself, out loud, "Stop it! This is nonsense! *She is your parents!*" And instantly, I find myself smiling and grateful for this almost religious illumination. Notice that I didn't say, "She is *like* your parents, or she is *like* your mother." I said, in the plural, "She is your parents!" In other words, she is the embodiment of my parents, of all parents. But what is especially meaningful to me is that she is, at this very moment of being, in America, the *only* manifestation of my parents, who are old and feeble and whom I love so much that if anyone were to be rude to them or impatient with them for being slow drivers or slow walkers, I would want to kill them.

Unfortunately, such moments do not last; and *until* we live in a world where the color of our skin is as trivial and personal a matter as the color of our undershorts, we Indians, the fairer-skinned among us especially, need to remember that we are *not* whites, even more than we are not blacks — and for much deeper reasons than our variable melanin concentrations. Thanks to our common history of colonialism, we Indians are closer to "Orientals" and to black people than we are to whites. It is important to make this distinction, and to recognize and understand the forces that make us, when we immigrate to Western countries, often internalize the harsher racism of white people towards black people of African origin.

The best answer to the color question on a bureaucratic form, or to someone asking the question on the phone, is an absurd one, such as "wheat with tones of burnt umber and an overlay of sienna" or "human." Or, considering that the dominant cultural equation today is the attempt by the nonwhites to impress the whites, perhaps the world can simply be divided into two groups: the Impressors and the Impressees. However, if forced at gunpoint to choose a color — black, white, or yellow, with no other choice — I would choose black. With all my heart.

Meanwhile, if I were to be asked my opinion of Cher's new breasts (and why shouldn't I be, having written at considerable length on various portions of the female anatomy?), I will answer, "I oppose them."

"Why?" my questioner wishes to know. "What wrong have those much-discussed, much-admired mammary glands done to you?"

"Because they are *there*," I reply. "On the front pages. Like the Monica Lewinsky circus and her thong underwear, taking up valuable space, newsprint, reportorial time, and public attention, and taking people's minds off starving children, injustice and stifling racial discrimination in America, and how three-fourths of the world lives."

Yes, let the forces that made Monica Lewinsky the most famous fellatrix in world history use a fraction of their ingenuity to ensure the supply of penicillin and vitamins for children in need. And a tiny fraction of print space devoted to her exploits (or even her underwear) to commenting on understanding other cultures and peoples, including, on occasion, reading and commenting on books that have *not* been written for Your benefit or for Your reading pleasure.

PART II: BROWN? STICK AROUND

The West, then, appears to me as a juggernaut which crushes people and cultures for insensate reasons.
— Serge Latrouche, The Westernization of the World.

SALMAN AND ME

"Religion for me has always meant Islam. I am able now to say that I am a Muslim; it is a source of happiness to say that I am . . . ."
— Salman Rushdie, in *The New York Times,* 1991

I wish I could say, Salman Who? But in my own way, being a self-exiled Indian writer with a claim to my own voice, I have had a rather intimate relationship with him in the last decade or so (and not of my own choice, for I really would have preferred a 36-24-36 blonde). I have stood about ten tentative feet from him as he peddled his novel *Shame* at the Asia Society in New York in 1986 — though, despite being a complete unknown at the time (compared to the internationally published and televised near-unknown now), I declined to join the autograph seekers' line, preferring simply to marvel at the Mughal princely looks and skin texture of the Indian, the bloody wog and heathen who had miraculously avatared into the blue-eyed boy of the Western literary establishment, reportedly thumping the table in anger for having been denied the second Booker that was rightfully his.

I will even confess that I have had to suffer his barging into my dreams, his cold and superior manner a reproof to my shy love (but lately, he's been getting warmer and more talkative). Further, I have been tagged with the unwelcome, headlined description, "THE RUSHDIE OF CATHOLICISM"; and for years after the fatwa, I was asked by nearly every Western Tom, Dick, and Harriet, who had just discovered that I was an Indian writer with a nearly-finished novel: "Not planning to be another Rushdie, are you, heh heh? Better watch your back!" Not unnaturally, considering my risky and forthright writing style, I have suffered my own personal fatwaphobia. Finally, I have met some people who knew him when he was a kid in Bombay, a Bombay poet once telling me, "Rushdie was here a few years back, and he was sitting exactly where you are sitting now." I've met others who no doubt break bread with him at regular intervals.

But the closest that I got to actually *being* Salman Rushdie was on a bright, rain-washed morning in a sliver of rainforest lodged in the heart of Puerto Rico. At a bungalow-like guest house kept by a local, long-suffering aristocrat named Imelda and her equally long-suffering Swedish companion Helga, I met a fellow tourist with perfect California cool, a well-tanned, perfect-bodied man who knew his wines, his hot tubs, and his Zen meditations as well as I knew my coconut curries. I informed him, when asked, that my name was Richard Crasta.

"But, but," he said, with the touching innocence many Westerners — and far too many Indians, for that matter — have about India's religious diversity, "What is your *real* name?"

I suddenly had a wicked impulse. With a little effort, I even managed for a second to counterfeit that superior, world-famous satanic glint in my eyes. "I really am Salman Rushdie," I said, in a tone of pained confession. "Don't tell anybody. I am traveling under an assumed name. You understand?"

The American looked at me with widening eyes, which were soon clouded by a light mist of bottomless compassion. "Oh, God," he said. "It really *is* you!" He swallowed, still not taking his eyes from me. Then he added, "Mr. Rushdie, I want to tell you I have great respect for what you are doing!"

I couldn't maintain my composure much longer. After all, how often does a mere mortal attain Rushdiehood?

Because, truth be told, I once delighted in him and in his work. Even though not many can truthfully claim they have read *Midnight's Children* or *Satanic Verses* to the end, or at least without occasionally dozing off, we young Indian writers felt liberated by his having stretched the English language the way a rhinoceros would stretch a

Sheik. Or at least for having blended into its turgid forms a Mumbaiite patois, which resulted in a refreshing linguistic biriyani that was good public relations for hitherto ghettoized and invisible Indian writers. Had he had a listed telephone number, I might have called to say, with Stevie Wonder-like simplicity, "I just called/to say/I love your books." And now, after a break of perhaps half a dozen years, I do admire the man again — everything I read about him, his godawful intellect and his joie de vivre, makes me admire him more. And even if some envy creeps into the following (and how can I, a human, be totally free of envy), I must compensate for the perceived envy by saying that his books (those I have read) have been among the most brilliant reading experiences of my life, often making me savor his sentences again and again.

But it would also be honest to admit that for a few years after the Saladdin days of the late Eighties, things happened that cooled my enthusiasm, my Salmandrine fires, by a few degrees. Even though, he is, as a writer, not just a heavy, but a heavy industry, while I am a cottage industry with a solitary, creaky spinning wheel. (Indeed, he not only belongs to the High Church of Literature, he could easily, with a little nose surgery, pass for an Anglican Archbishop.)

A year or so after the fatwa (which had made me join an anti-fatwa march in New York), I had nearly finished my novel and developed some confidence — or perhaps, hubris — as a writer. In one of my most passionate columns for the Bombay (or Mumbai) daily, *The Independent*, I had vehemently supported Rushdie's cause, flaying my countrymen for having chickened out in his defense. However, recognizing a fellow incurable agnostic at a distance of four thousand miles, I had also briefly expressed my skepticism at the genuineness of The World's Most Famous Mumbaiite's just-announced "conversion" to Islam — an episode that he himself later apologized for as "an embarrassing flirtation with Islam." Unfortunately, the paper ran my piece under the caption, "WHO BELIEVES SALMAN RUSHDIE?" — overruling my own submitted title, "A Pro-Rushdie Indian Speaks."

There had been a personal reason for my passion in Rushdie's defence, as well as my disappointment with his "conversion." I saw myself as a victim of a locally corrupted Indian Catholicism that had transformed my early life, and my parents' entire lives, into a hell of self-torture and fear of damnation. Thanks to it, I will be wracked by guilt forever (and I deserve it, because I have *sinned!*). To hold that a man should not express strong opinions about the religion that fenced in his rightful boyhood joys with religious barbed wire, that cut short his childhood, scarred his emotions, and twisted his mind . . . to say that he should doff his topi or hat to the system that cruelly squashed him and made him refrain from pulling girls' ponytails . . . it was an outrage.

I quote a few lines from my computer file copy of this essay:

"As a fellow writer from a generation of Indians that has grown up feeling powerless as an older generation of leaders, fanatics, and narrow-minded communalists scuttle the glorious possibilities that free India represented, and for whom, empowered by Western literary traditions of freedom, black humor and satire are essential and sometimes the only possible language of expression, Rushdie's fate has been and is personally important to me. Even if I hadn't found a pointer to Rushdie's own vision in *The Satanic Verses* ("A poet's work: to name the unnamable, to point out frauds, to take sides, to start arguments, shape the world and stop it from going to sleep") . . . I have been with Rushdie 100 percent ever since this controversy began; I believe his right to artistic self-expression is absolute, *whatever* his intent and meaning in *The Satanic Verses*. After all, all ideas worth their salt are by definition a criticism or a denial of competing ideas. . . Now when I hear the latest news . . . Give me a break, fellas. I'd sooner believe that Bertrand Russell had suddenly become a born-again Christian, passing 'Jesus Saves' buttons to acidheads in Washington Square Park."

So I, a fellow rebel, was a little disappointed that the man had bowed before the thing he feared and rebelled against. My only other less-than-adoring observation in my essay was a truly believed and passionately felt comment about Rushdie's sexual prudishness, which my novel's narrator sees as an un-Indian trait that was imposed on us from without: "He still wears his Victorian knickers." (I had just kicked off mine, you see, and mine had been longer and thicker than his, his probably being muslin see-throughs woven by Bengali serfs; and my number one rule as a writer was that I had to be *honest*, for god's sake! And golly, was I proud of my accomplishment!)

That was the last column I published in *The Independent*. The paper, which had been publishing everything I sent them verbatim, never published me again, never cared to inform me of their decision, and never even paid me for my last few columns. Thus did that chapter end (until the paper itself came to an end about three years later, when divine justice struck a blow for writers not paid their dues).

Human beings, perplexed by circumstances, sometimes latch on to far-fetched explanations, particularly if they are ex-Catholics with still-buried fears of heavenly damnation — as an examination of my fellow lapsed Catholic James Joyce's biography amply demonstrates. Joyce-like, I fantasized outlandish scenarios. Such as: Had "Who Believes In Salman Rushdie?" been perhaps mailed to the literary god Rushdie by a chela, a spittoon bearer to his aristocratic family, or even by his mother with the note, "*Dekho beta, kya kya bhol rahe hain, Bombaiwalleh log!*"? *Look, son, what all these Bombay people are talking and writing!* Did Rushdie, in turn, thunder on the intercontinental telephone line to the *Independent* editor: "Who is the nincompoop who wrote this drivel? How *dare* he imply, even mildly, that I am a liar?" Did the trembling Bombay editor (we Indians, like our British brethren, tend to get weak-kneed in the presence of the celebrated, it's in our genetic makeup) say, "Begging your pardon, Sir! He won't be published in this town again!"

It was only for a few moments, during a period of great strain, that I entertained this deliciously crazy, paradoxical, nonsensical, and totally absurd notion that the world's most famous victim of attempted ultimate censorship and automatic world champion of free speech or his self-appointed protectors had stooped to censoring "lesser" writers. I repeat: totally absurd, even if a few remarkable coincidences might have made me and a cocaine-sniffing Sherlock Holmes suspicious. Such as the coincidence that none of my two or three attempts to write for Indian papers was successful right after that. In the top American publications, I of course had no reason to hope, being not as "good" as the Bright (Light) Brown Boys with their Oxford-lightening creams; being too brown, too prickly, too politically incorrect, my rough native edges and my colonial anger un-sandpapered by an upper class, Oxbridge education, had no place ("No place for this in our current mix" was the euphemistically stock but unwittingly honest Freudian slip of a response from one magazine, making me exclaim: "There will never be a place for me in the mix of this world.")

I forgot all about this incident, as my novel, about which I was rather cockily excited and hopeful, reached completion and began to flirt with acceptance by the powerful. A few years thereafter, an East European immigrant in New York, after reading my novel and reacting rapturously to its honesty and its different take on the immigrant experience, offered a rather startling and paranoid theory about why the book, despite nearly fanatic enthusiasm from my British acquiring editor (who lost his job shortly thereafter, through another monumental act of sheer coincidence), had neither been lionized by the British literary establishment nor been accepted by American publishers. "You see, Rushdie is a sacred cow for the British and for the West. Your article implied that his conversion to Islam was suspect. At that time, the issue was still hot. They might have thought you were endangering his life by your statement."

Her hypothesis fascinated me, simply because of its deranged absurdity. A satirical writer — that is, a professional attacker of sacred cows — attacks another culture's sacred cow, and thus becomes a sacred cow himself (a true Moo-Salman indeed), one whom it is forbidden to attack. Still, how could my puny article implying untrue Mussalmanship (or a fake "conversion") in a relatively elite Bombay spinoff of London's *Independent* be considered as endangering Rushdie the international sacred cow? Perhaps indeed the paper was on the Ayatollah's reading list, being flown to him every morning from Bombay?

No, I don't buy her conspiratorial hypothesis, or any significant role for Rushdie, or even his secret supporters, in my fate. But at the time, feeling a little apologetic about the *Independent*'s taunting headline, I wrote a breezy letter to Rushdie, assuring him of my support (I can imagine the sighs of relief in his various castle and motel hideouts, the aphrodisiac effect of the good news on his lovemaking being immediately noticed by assorted grateful literary blondes) and enclosing an excerpt from my recently rebuffed novel.

I might have had better luck pretending I was a blonde bombshell — for I received no reply.

But after the publication of my British edition, at moments when I was high on love and universal brotherhood and my confidence in my novel's quality (and heartened by its rosy reception in India a few months back), I again hoped that Rushdie, who has given enthusiastic blurbs to many a powerful Western novelist who could have survived without his praise, would have the courage and the nobility to come out and say on behalf of a fellow risk-taker, "I don't agree with all the sentiments expressed in *The Revised Kama Sutra*, especially its unflattering picture of my beloved, poop-filled Mumbai . . . but the old boy has balls, you must admit! Given that he didn't go to Cambridge or have a superrich pop, ha ha!"

As history will not note, that didn't happen. And I understand. Put yourself in Shahenshah Salman's Size 13 shoes if you can. If you were he, a lonely Shahenshah with no brown social equal, would you not prefer the company of thrice-born Martin Amis and an armful of chicks and a bathtub full of champagne ferried in by British Secret Service agents to the company of Richard Crasta dolefully exhuming the corpse of colonialism? He was making the cent-per-cent correct choice, yaar. What do you think, his Poppa became wealthy by doling out scholarships to Bombay slumdwellers?

Meanwhile, he was on the upswing again. He came out with *The Moor's Last Sigh,* and it was clear that despite his earlier proclivity towards a cartoonish, Hindi-filmi depiction of Indian Christians — he seemed to satirize the Indian Christians of his bygone Bombay days for not being as successful at achieving whiteness as he himself now has — he had recovered from his depression, and his imagination was un-stopped. As for his social life, his following, and His Sacred Mooship: he was chewing the ambrosial cud in Immortal City. At this very time, I, the Writer of the Mournful Countenance, quite deservedly hadn't been published in either America or Burundi, though I was into my third edition in India and my second in the U.K.; why should I, a professed anti-imperialist, be published by the Powers That Ruled the World? That was when a brilliant but devilish American friend, himself unpublished and therefore subversive, whispered in my ears this Satanic hypothesis: "Rushdie is a false hero. He attacked the people we hate, so we love him. You attacked *us*, so we do not." He was reflecting a widespread American skepticism about the justification for Rushdie's status — some going to the extent of believing it was a well-planned career move. Even more provocatively, he was suggesting that the West had polished Salman's missile and pointed it at the Muslim world.

All bosh of course (though I must tell you that there are people out there who secretly think and say these things, and that not all Indians, whatever their religion, have merrily jumped onto the Rushdie bandwagon). And now for a little more bosh, now that we're on a roll with it: what Indian writers like Rushdie, Arundhati Roy, and Vikram Seth do is to have a Mother Teresa effect on Western understanding and attention. Thanks to the Western media's need for simplified images and symbols of the complex East (over which they cannot afford to spend too much time, since they have Princess Diana, Monica Lewinsky, and Michael Jackson to study and digest), these trumpeted writers *become* India, they *become* the Western view and experience of India.

The grizzly, unkempt, un-suave, uncomfortably male and political, and uncategorizable writings of Indian-language writers such as Shivaram Karanth and O.P. Vijayan, and of lower-class, courageous, cliché-exploding, writers such as Kiran Nagarkar (author of *Ravan and Eddie*), Swapan K. Biswas, Kancha Ilaiah (author of *Why I am Not a Hindu*), Dr. B.R. Ambedkar, gives the lie to the idea that half a dozen Oxbridge-educated upper class voices from four major cities can presume to speak for one billion Indians.

When you add the Chitra Diwakarunis and the Suitable Babes, the beautiful exotic ones whose images get splashed across *The New York Times* as the new find, even white women writers start getting miffed (some of my white women friends have admitted this, and shame on them, even if they are my friends). Leading one to ask: Will the West's tolerance for diversity, for truly new voices (after all, these were both Oxbridge-shaped or Oxbridge-shaved or McOxbridge-fertilized intellects) be exhausted before other writers had their say? Will future Indian writers, both the true originals and the approximately one thousand hopeful and 1,500-page *Also Suitable Boys* (I predict: *The Suit-and-Bootable Boy, The Shootable Boy, The Suitable Bhaiyya, The Suitable Bhenji, The Suitable Bore,* and a few other titles in R-rated territory*)* that I predict will give rise to a fair number of hernias among Western editors about four years from now, have to revert to their old condition of neglect and poverty, like many a Third World archaeological monument? Possibly they will, unless they are sanctified by inclusion in Il Papa Rushdie's anthologies of Indian writing — Salman Rushdie in his benighted old age and pashahood being Her Majesty's new Gurkha or gatekeeper or headmistress of Indian writing (like the nun whose job it is to lift the skirts of her charges to check if they are wearing clean knickers or no knickers), keeping out the bad boys and admitting only the well-behaved (those suitable for the delicate appetites of the Exalted Western sahibs and fainting-prone memasahibs).

And finally (I reach deep into my soul here): How can I not think of Salman Rushdie, at least sometimes? My writings could upset some oversensitive fatwaist, even tomorrow, some fatwaist who wakes up to a To-Do list on his refrigerator, a list he had composed the night before:

1. Get milk.
2. Attend PTA and flog impious teachers, tots, and parents.
3. Issue a fatwa against R.C.

It would be dishonest for me to pretend that the thought has never crossed my mind. And strangely, though I have been anxious to protect my freedom and that of my family's, there have been those brief dark moments when a fatwa has seemed preferable to having my writing ignored. Let's admit it: a fatwa is the greatest career advancement tool ever invented, better even than fellating the entire Nobel Committee.

Having expressed the forbidden and the fatwa-able, just because I do not approve of literary cowardice from ex-colonial writers, even in myself, let me end by saying: Rushdie is a great talent, especially from Midnight till Satanic, and I wish him a full and productive life. Especially because, even with just one-tenth of his productivity, I function as much at the frontiers of free and endangered speech as he does — or erroneously *imagine* that I do, for my writings wouldn't even offend a cloistered nun (well, they would; but nuns don't issue fatwas). In which imaginary case, free speech is even more important to me, because his writings are *already* assured of immortality.

THE NEW SPIRITUAL COLONIALISM

On a Greek island overrun by German tourists, in a hotel where the blue sky meets a rust-colored beach backed by a manicured lawn dotted with palms and Muzak-oozing rocks, I met a female German tourist at a bar. We introduced ourselves, and then I showed her the German edition of my novel, which I was carrying around to get some live reactions to the book, so I could try to understand the German response. She examined the book, laughed appreciatively for about two minutes at some of its opening pages, and then skimmed through the latter half for two more minutes. Returning the book, she remarked, with some disappointment in her voice, "But this is not *spiritual*." She added, after a pause, "I admire India because it is *spiritual*. Gandhi! The Dalai Lama!" She also mentioned another author of spiritual texts, unfamiliar to me. (Thankfully, it was not T. Lobsang Rampa.)

Her companion corrected her gently, telling her that the Dalai Lama and the other author she had mentioned were Tibetans. The woman had lumped India, Tibet, and the entire "East" into one porous entity.

"But India, it is spiritual," my critic insisted.

"But *I* am not," I retorted. "And millions of my educated, younger countrymen are not. Many of us are people in whose lives religion does not play a major or overriding role. Many of us, who observe the small-mindedness of the religious folks and fanatics around us, are sick of religion. We are sick of people fighting and killing each other in the name of religion. We have too much religion! We are in rebellion against it. Why can't we? Don't we have a right to? Indeed, some of us even call ourselves atheists, agnostics, or rationalists."

She repeated her point about the beauty of India's spirituality — which I perceived as a rebuke to my un.

I thought: You discount my humanity, my uniqueness, my individuality, my right to create and recreate myself at every moment — the right you ferociously demand for yourselves. If I don't meet the stereotype you have created in your bloody ignorance for people of my race or national origin (yes, it is national origin, not current citizenship), I am dispensable, nonexistent. You disappear me if I cannot be conveniently compartmentalized.

Either we are spiritualists, or we're doctors and computer scientists, or cultural exotics, or maharajas, or barbarians and oppressors of women. One billion Indians: couldn't you possibly make space in your heads for more than five categories of Indian men? Not even Spitters, Shitters, Beggars, and Naked Fakirs?

Even Gandhi: he was far more complex than a mere spiritual symbol. He was a nationalist, a fighter for justice, a man who challenged the West — and sometimes, his own body. He had naked women sleep by his side so he could test his self-control, you know. Just like you, to reduce the complex Gandhi to an uncomplicated holy man.

We understand that you suffer from spiritual hunger, that your civilization leaves you feeling empty inside. But don't pass on to our frail Eastern shoulders the burden of your gaping void [no sexual meaning intended, honest], your superficiality. We do not want to be punished for your failure to be happy, or to be condemned to spiritual colonialism. Think: there has to be something earthy about us, we have to be doing some fucking some time (even if they're quickies), or else we wouldn't exist.

In fact, I have news for you. Many of us educated Indians, having run our own rat race, also feel empty. We're in the same boat as you, so let's share the rowing. We refuse to be your spiritual Gunga Dins, refuse to wipe your asses with our perfumed spiritual tissues. Just because you are suddenly weary of spreading your legs for every bloke with a hardon, you have decided you want to be spiritual, right?

If you really desire to be spiritual, if you really wish to be pure spirit, the only guaranteed method is to donate all your wealth and most of your income (except what you need to survive show up at your jobs) to the poor millions in the Third World countries. When sufficient numbers of you do that, and for long enough, perhaps, one day, the situation might be reversed, and the world will witness the phenomenon of rich, pot-bellied Easterners and Nepali Sherpas ascending the Alps seeking spiritual enlightenment and the meaning of life from *The Pink Sages of Early Neanderthal Wisdom* — while you formerly well-heeled Westerners, are now reduced to being their human donkeys, carrying their rations and their toilet paper on your malnourished backs.

What exactly are Westerners who say, "You're Eastern, you are spiritual," implying? That a Western constitution is inherently incapable of spirituality? Admittedly, spirituality is not woven into the fabric of the Western way of life, as it is in a traditional society such as Bali — at least on the surface of things. Many Westerners (G.W. Bush for example), thanks to the mind-body divide or their capacity for compartmentalization, can claim to be Christians even while the pursuit of self-interest is the only game in town. "Love your enemy as yourself" must be the line that the Pentagon uses for laughs as it rains thousands of smart "love" bombs on civilian targets in the currently targeted country destined for a CNN fireworks display; for the West has quarantined its spirituality within the walls of its churches, convents, and monasteries. Western evangelists may try to export "their" Christian religion, but it is far more likely that you will witness a living example of the Sermon on the Mount in some poor Asian or African village where a poor man with nothing to eat offers his last piece of bread to a stranger — something that will never, never, not even after ten million years of Power yoga classes, meditation retreats, and New Age workshops, ever happen in the West. So the West should stop dictating to the East the behavior it considers proper and suitable for it. The West should try not to imagine the world as if it were a Whitehound bus in which, when you decide it is time to sit on your arse and become spiritual, you leave the driving to us, your Oriental slaves and Spiritual Gunga Dins.

You see the problem? You are telling us who we are, and who we ought to be. Once upon a time, we were savages, and we needed to be Christianized in order to be saved. Today, we are Hindus: even if we've been baptized or circumcised, so long as we're from India, we're Hindus in your eyes. Therefore, for the ease of your digestions, we had better call ourselves Arundhati Roy, not Suzanne Roy [see Endnotes]; Avatar Prabhu, not Richard Crasta; or else, you'll have nothing to do with us. And, being Hindoos and holy-cow-worshipers, we need to work overtime at being spiritual so as to provide you some Spiritual Chicken Soup to give you strength and nourishment you need in the intervals between your smart-bombing runs on naughty brown nations. It's the same old story: once again, you are defining us, and by doing so, are denying us our freedom.

It's quite likely that if Gandhi hadn't been "spiritual," celibate, and vegetarian (in addition to his many other distinctions and qualities of character), but a cigar-chomping, cognac-swilling, ballsy and blustery tough-talker like Churchill, Indians would still be in the British Empire, still be washing their white masters' underwear. But why apply this "spiritual" standard to all of one billion people just because we are brown and, on average, a little shorter than you?

Nor was my experience with the German tourist the only one of its kind. On an Air India flight from Tokyo to Delhi, I talked to a young Frenchman who had recently visited China and was greatly upset. Why? Because the modern Chinese were not as spiritual as he had been primed by the Western media to expect, not walking around with books by Lao Tzu, and beginning their sentences with "The Tao of ...." In fact, these bloody, fucking Chinamen with their 30 million cell phones were as materialistic as . . . as . . . *as he was*!

He was blaming the Chinese for their jeans, their cell phones, their digital traffic lights, and their focus on making money, when Rupert Murdoch's lust for profits had in fact beamed STAR TV or satellite television to Asian villages and transformed people's outlooks. Half-naked and barefoot villagers in remote parts of India had begun to

spend anxious nights worrying about, of all things, their *bad breath* —
because capitalist commercials had effectively penetrated their
ancient, spiritual, breath-free minds.

Spiritual and exotic: these are two of the tags that oppress us.
Perhaps it is true that the "spiritual" tag is applied more to the Hindu
countries of the world (India, Nepal, and the island of Bali) and to
certain Buddhist nations such as Tibet and Thailand, than it is to
Moslem countries; but exotic defines us all, perhaps with the
exception of those among us who have baptized away our exoticism
by means of an Oxford or Cambridge education.

Maybe you want us to be spiritual, but not sexy, because in some
secret antechamber of your minds, you wish for us to limit our
existence to the minimum possible number that will serve your
purposes, decontaminate your computer systems of Y2K bugs, and
cheaply transcribe your medical records at Third World sweatshop
rates (the Merriam-Webster Thesaurus provides the following
synonyms for "spiritual": bodiless, disembodied, nonphysical). You
don't like the idea of a sexy male Indian, because you worry that
there are already too many Indians in the world, and you don't want
us making any more little Indians — or half-Indians.

Madams and Messieurs: I and my countless colored brothers
demand our humanity. We demand that you hear us, and allow us the
same rights that you give yourselves. We demand that you see us as
we are, whether spiritual or "non-spiritual", whether Hindu or
Buddhist, whether theistic or agnostic. We refuse to perform
monkey-dances for your pleasure.

And what makes you think we cannot be spiritual and sexy at the
same time? That is your own hang-up. We've become prisoners of
your racist, little-minded ideology. We are invisible to you. Either we
are what you want to see in us, or we don't exist.

In my book, *Beauty Queens, Children and the Death of Sex*, I suggest
that this forced labeling of the Eastern male as "spiritual" (a code
word for "not sexy", "not assertive," "not demanding full payment
for services rendered") is not as accidental or innocuous as it sounds,
but part of the colonial program, which has simply become more

subtle. Yes, it is part of the program of Divide and Conquer, because power likes to perpetuate itself, because human beings have an urge to dominate other human beings and other races — except when checked by their conscience, by an impassioned appeal for fairness by a respected figure, or by open revolt or relentless exposure. The program is in operation everywhere, including in the publishing world: witness the award of the Nobel Prize to Toni Morrison but not to Ralph Ellison, or the extra cash bonuses for Indian women writers and film-makers who will dish dirt on Indian males. In its choice of the Eastern writers it will patronize — or not patronize — Western publishing is only following the traditional strategy of conquerors towards a conquered race: unsex the men, "liberate" the women, reward and honor the eunuchs or race-traitors, thus letting them keep their untamed brothers in check. If the conquered women and men don't get along as a result, so much the better, for Divide and Conquer still works, though the modern-day colonial lust is for minds, hearts, and bodies, not land. Once upon a time, Divide and Rule meant causing divisions between one prince and another, or one religious group and another, and thus ensuring a cheap flow of spices and raw materials to the West. Now, it means dividing men against women, and it serves the conqueror race well, ensuring an uninterrupted flow of more cheap secretaries, masseuses, housekeepers, governesses, and erotic assistants from the former colonies.

Take an example of this double standard. If a brown woman dreams of passion, as in Shobha De's novels or Namita Gokhale's *Paro: Dreams of Passion* (published by Chatto & Windus), it's okay, it's, whooaaaaaaaaa . . . a wet dream! The admittedly beautiful Shobha De, who some deride as an Indian Jackie Collins or even as a soft porn queen without much depth to her characters or her dialogue, even succeeded in getting her books on the curriculum at an Australian university. A male Indian writer learns that he better stick to suitable or literary fiction, or else he'll get nowhere outside *Debonair* and *Fantasy*, the two sadly battered Indian men's magazines (the editors have often been arrested with copies seized by police), which pay their contributors just about enough to cover a few meals at a good restaurant, and which anyway prefer that their fiction steer clear of politics, which I cannot. The neutered or sanitized men of the conquered race thus pose no threat to the women of the Master Race, while the empowered women of the conquered race present exciting potential trophies to the men of the Master Race.

So don't talk to me about Vikram Seth, who is as unthreatening as Pearl Buck, or about Salman Rushdie, who, having admitted to having an eye on the Nobel, perhaps realizes he must be on very, very good behavior until he gets his reward (and after that, I admit, I do have some slight hopes for him; he's my boy!). There are really not many well known *living* colored writers who write in a fiery style and stand tall (in English, that is; we do have a few in the local languages, but they are never translated — even rebellion in the local languages has its price). We are so powerless, that we've in general taken the cue and followed the program you've set for us.

Maybe this is because the sort of courage and generosity and true open-mindedness among white editors, which existed in the Forties, Fifties, and Sixties, when Richard Wright, James Baldwin, Malcolm X and Ralph Ellison were writing and were published, do not exist anymore. Maybe the West is so jaded, and has so self-hypnotized itself into believing in the post-racial and post-racist society of its fantasies that Western editors don't even want to pretend to be true and just anymore. Maybe they decided, "We have these four black male Big Guys, and a couple of Brown Big Guys (Salman being one of them), and we've given them their voice. That's it. No more strong colored men. Now we'll give their women power, and start painting their men as oppressors. That'll take care of them, as well as keep *our* feminists busy and mollified, for a while."

Sorry, folks, that turkey won't fly. The truth of the world, the truth of our lives, is not as simple as that. In my next novel, I plan to introduce you to a few oppressed colored men, including a battered colored man. I will also introduce to you a black woman who said to me on an airplane (all my best conversations take place in midair, I ought to be made a honorary member of the Mile-High Club), "I feel sorry for black men. They have it so hard. If an equally qualified black man and I were to go for a job interview, I would get the job. Absolutely without doubt."

But that's another story: I mean, that's another novel. For now, just try a little thought trick: imagine all the sexes were changed, that an exotic brown babe wrote a novel about a battered female . . . and just offer me one-fourth of the publishing advance that you would offer a suitable babe, will you?

A footnote: My German-language publisher did a fine job publishing me, even putting a gorgeous Rajasthani belle on the jacket, but probably faced some resistance from the spirituality-seeking readership that would normally even bother to consider reading a non-spiritual Indian author, especially if he openly admitted to owning a (not easily subdued) penis. The next year (out of pure coincidence, and not to atone for publishing a bad brown boy the previous year, I am sure), they published Manju Kapoor's *Difficult Daughters*. Kapoor's distinctly greater success (she had a multiple-city reading tour in Europe, whereas I had had just two days in Frankfurt) had her beaming at the press and publishing audience at a swanky Frankfurt hotel; she gushed with true charm and honesty (My first impressions of her are of a likeable, genuine person).

"I don't know whether I should say this," she said, barely suppressing her giggles. "Tee hee."

"Oh, please do, please do," the audience chanted.

"All the [Indian] male characters in my novel are jerks! Ha ha!"

The audience roared in laughter, whereas I sat there as if hit by a lightning bolt of understanding. To Asian female novelists wishing to succeed in the West, even to black female novelists who had subliminally been following the Alice Walker prescription of making colored women the victims of their monstrous men, she had uttered a formula as profound as: $E=mc^2$.

HOW TO BE AN INVISIBLE AUTHOR
or, How I Escaped Fame and Booker

[An earlier version of this satire, springing from my enthusiastic British editor's decision to nominate my novel on behalf of his publishing company for the Booker Prize, was published in *India Today* under the title "Dodging The Booker," shortly after the Booker Awards of 1994]

It is time for some of you to bring out your champagne glasses, folks, and join me in celebration (oh, don't be shy, let me pour)! My novel's narrow escape from mention in the just-out Booker Prize shortlist has ensured that for at least a few weeks longer, I can bask in happy oblivion, content as a cow all alone in a lush green meadow on a warm summer day. Indeed, my novel, to the bafflement of my once-salivating publishers, has generated not an iota of frenzy save a few pleasant radio interviews now floundering about the Milky Way along with the shouts of fishwives.

Ah, Oblivion — how footstompingly fortunate! No tabloid or Sunday magazine exclusives, with photographers snapping me in star-spangled swimwear while I grin sheepishly, sprawled on a lounger at a five-star hotel swimming pool! No reporters thrusting their microphones into my face, begging for quotable quotes! No television images of me being hustled out of my apartment by smiling publicists and grim security amazons into waiting limousines.

Just what I was secretly praying for. Narrowly, but decisively, I have escaped the burden that is Fame, the cruel burden that Marlon Brando eloquently lashes out against in an installment of his forthcoming autobiography published in a once hoity-toity newspaper whose feature space is increasingly hogged by the cosmic and carnal moans of fat cat celebrities. With all those Booker shortlisters and near-shortlisters for reporters and critics to bother and analyze, I am now *guaranteed* at least a few more months, if not a few more decades, of nameless anonymity, of bird-like freedom, of *life*, of being denied reservations in *middlebrow* restaurants, of being harassed by terrorist-nosing cops merely for walking the Caucasian earth.

Which is what I really, truly wanted all along (notice all those taunting, subversive provocations in my novel, designed to piss off any misty-eyed do-gooders who might try to bestow me with fame?). For who wants to walk the world in constant terror of being recognized, wearing dark glasses in cloudy weather, changing mustache styles or beard styles, phobic of picking one's nose, petrified of accidentally letting up an explosive epithet or two, terrified of stumbling before a lurking camera and being pinned down as human? The perils of fame are, of course, somewhat mitigated if you have a well-fortified bungalow at the top of Mulholland Drive and four wives and countless mistresses — except when they sue you for palimony, which is of course great news for your lawyers, who must be chuckling all the way down the slopes of Beverly Hills to their bank vaults. But fame without such celestial perks? Deliver me from it, Oh Lord!

Besides, those tempting strumpets Fame and Fortune pose unacceptable risks for one who writes in disturbing and unconventional territory (i.e. the Unsuitable). For what if I was to lose the very wellspring of my creativity, my passion, and my commitment: my outsiderness? It is a consummation devoutly to be wished away, or at least postponed until senility or white old age, whichever comes first. Consider: wouldn't it be tragic if my novel had "succeeded" wildly? Imagine the headlines in some patriotic Indian newspaper:

REBEL INDIAN AUTHOR SELLS OUT
EIGHT MONTHS AFTER INDIAN DEBUT!

Booker Prize Assured, Say Critics

"You can bet my writing will be more well-behaved and more respectful in future," Best-selling Phenomenon Richard Crasta assured a pinstriped literary gathering at Christ Church College, Oxford. "I am already working on an epicene version of *The Revised Kama Sutra* in which Vijay Prabhu is a cute butler at a British officer's bungalow in Simla and every other male Indian character is either a cartoonish villain, a menial, an incompetent, or a Dr. Aziz-ish sentimental buffoon. I'm also working on a Disney adaptation called *It's a Small Sutra After All.* Flogging the dead horses of colonialism might have got me here, but to tell the truth, we are all brothers, all God's chillun, and all this conflict-shor-flict is tosh, isn't it?"

Sad to say, it's 1757 all over again: the Battle of Plassey, in which Clive won India by offering a little baksheesh to the Nawab's general. By dangling their moolah before one of ours, the English have won once again. And India has lost an author who had specialized in the transformation of pain into thought-provoking parables of colonialism. Richard Crasta, hailed by Khushwant Singh as well as *The Times* of London — in exactly the same words — as "the new Seth and Rushdie rolled into one big head-popping reefer, the brown Henry Miller and voice of Third World Catholic Reformation, the author of the Magna Carta of Indian sexual liberation" will heretofore experience no more pain. Just holidays on the Riviera (the nude section), script conferences in Beverly Hills (the fashionable side), and parking his burgeoning rear in the overstuffed leather chairs of the Cambridge and Oxford Club (darkie section).

"You are my sunshine and my moonshine too," gushed Crasta, beaming at the dons, who (men and women both) in an unprecedented gesture of affection had flung their panties at him. "We Indians had better behave and get our condoms together and control our population; we have work to do, cheap clothes to sew for you, prawns to net for your tables." The standing ovation shattered some ancient stained glass windows, but Crasta's publisher, rejoicing in the sensation that has jolted her company into the Fortune 500, agreed to replace them with nuclear-proof plastic imitations.

By a Brahmin pigtail's breadth, and with a fantastic helping of luck, I have escaped the harrowing fate of Fame and Insiderness. Really, who wants that bunch of overrated grapes dangled by slutty Damsel Fortune? If you have even an iota of doubt, don't take my word for it. Ask my miserable pal and soul-brudder Salman Rushdie.

HOW TO WIN THE BOOKER PRIZE
A Shortlist of Dos and Don'ts for Indian/Nonwhite Writers

On cool reflection, many a colored writer might decide that it is
still far safer, infinitely more sensible, and a lot shrewder for him to
win a Booker (think of all the fame, the parties, the cold cash flowing
into Indian pockets) than to protect his voice and assert his freedom
to write as he pleases.

So, to my fellow Indians and Third Worlders too weak to resist
fame, I offer a shortlist of dos and don'ts: The Five Rules for
Winning the Booker.

Rule One: Attack as many Third World villains and blackies as
you wish, but thou shalt not attack the Masters of the Universe,
unless you are taking sides with the Liberal, the Longhaired or the
Pony-Tailed (of both sexes), wine drinking, Gucci-loafer wearing
Masters of the Media against Their Conservative Enemies.

Rule Two: Thou shalt not cast too-admiring glances on thy
Masters' Wives or Daughters, except under a permitted quota and
lottery system for PL-480 Surplus Daughters.

Rule Three: To would-be Brown Literati and Impresarios:
Colored clowns or indecisive and timid Dr. Azizes, colorful eunuchs,
and sex-neutral Sabus shall be tolerated and may even make it to
Hollywood or James Bond scripts or to sociological studies and films,
but do not create strong brown male characters unless they be dead,
completely neutered, or based on Good Dead Indians such as
Gandhi.

Rule Four: Never attack the Christian religion or establishment,
even if you are a Christian by birth. No matter that Martin Luther
and Bertrand Russell did it. You are not entitled.

Rule Five: Advice to satirists: Avoid satire, unless it is directed at your fellow-Indians, especially those who threaten the Masters. Better to aim for a Dickensian or Austenian *Passage to India* with some feminist finger-pointing and Indian gods (small gods included) thrown in. Yes, thou shalt be brave, fearless, and honest; but thou shalt not take on too big a Western target. To appear evenhanded in your satire without angering the Masters, follow the unobtrusive policy of a pencil flashlight: spotlight just one tiny square inch of Western darkness. Ignore the blooming night around you. And don't ever, ever try to frame its fearful symmetry.

* * *

That last line wasn't a bad place to end this chapter, except that this might be a good opportunity to present to my readers a nugget of high wisdom that HarperCollins India inadvertently left out of my previous book, *Beauty Queens, Children and the Death of Sex* (pardon any repetition in the next edition of that book). And what was the missing piece of high wisdom? While the jacket promises to reveal the Two Types of Indian (or Third World) Writing in English, the text cheats you of this promise. Literary critics, Indians, and fellow Third Worlders: lend me your ears.

Speaking of a Congressman, Lyndon Johnson once bragged, "I've got his pecker in my pocket." Meaning, he controlled him. This phrase is sometimes extended to describe the males from a subordinate social group who function on condition of keeping their sexuality hidden and unthreatening to the Master group. It is sometimes observed that a black celebrity is tolerated in the West so long as he keeps his pecker in his pocket.

Thus, the literature written by colored people writing in English and born after 1945, in the Age of Freud and Joyce's *Ulysses*, when the intertwining of the sexual and the apparently non-sexual in the human being gained near-universal acceptance, and sexual thoughts and desires became a legitimate subject for serious fiction, may be divided into two kinds:

1. Pecker-in-pocket literature, hijra literature, eunuch fiction, or suitable boy literature. PIP literature, in short. This includes some fine and deservedly praised and valuable and sometimes-great writing, and we need lots of it. However, any male sexuality in it is quite subdued, weak, or self-derisive. To put it quite bluntly, the outstanding practitioners of this literature write as if the West has their peckers in its pocket (admittedly, that must be a pretty big pocket, or those must be pretty small peckers). Luckily for Indian women writers, they don't suffer from this problem, because Mother Nature didn't give them any peckers to begin with. I arbitrarily assign a 1940 cutoff date (of birth) to exclude great writers such as R.K. Narayan and Raja Rao, who belong to a more buttoned-up and Lingam-Shy age, and cannot be blamed for being pre-Midnight's children.

2. Literature that isn't pecker-in-pocket. Or pecker-positive literature (PPL in short). While there are many writers in the Indian languages who belong in this category, and whose names for the general reader are a jumble of unfamiliar syllables (E.V.K. Periyar, Cho Ramaswamy, O.P.Vijayan, Kamala Das), and some journalists or former journalists writing in English (R.K. Karanjia, Baburao Patel, Khushwant Singh — Shobha De being a contentious candidate), it is hard to find many who write in English (the few exceptions include lower-caste writers such as Swapan K. Biswas and Kancha Ilaiah, pecker-positive literature including not only reproductively unrepressed writing, but also courageous writing.[10]

Why is this so? If we had been talking of just a few individual modern writers being pecker-shy, you might have explained it as a matter of their personal choice, but when it describes a large tribe, it smacks of our have willingly surrendered our manhood in return for

---

[10] I define "courageous" writing as writing that makes you tremble to write it, making you fear the possible wrath of society, your family, or your god — but that you will still not withhold from publication, because of your higher duty to express your truth.

that Divine (i.e. white) approval and a fistful of pennies. Our Anglophilia, particularly that of our intellectual leaders, keeps us a neutered country, and being neutered is not a healthy way for a country to be, though it may be the choice of a few specific individuals, who have discovered that it is a very profitable occupation.

But more on Anglophilia in the chapter, "No More Head." Meanwhile, if you want to even dream of winning a Booker, be absolutely certain to you keep your dickie in your docket . . . I mean, your wickie in your wocket . . . I mean, your pen-knife in its plastic jacket.

IMPRESSING WHITE TOURISTS IN INDIA

It was a pleasantly crisp winter evening, with fog rolling over the hills, wisps of it rubbing up against the large glass window panes of the Karnataka State Tourism Development Corporation restaurant in Nandi Hills, the hill station that rises above the Deccan Plateau of South India like a benign blue growth. Lights twinkled on in the numerous villages of the valley below us as the evening quickly changed to dusk, and dusk changed into the dark of tropical night. I had picked a strategic seat that would allow me to take in a panoramic view of the valleys and the Nandi temple, while simultaneously enabling me to indulge in my pastime of people watching. I had ordered a dinner of vegetable fried rice, a safe dish for this restaurant, which has to fetch its scarce orders of meat from the valley below or from the city of Bangalore some forty miles away. After my meal, I would head back to my room to write. I had come there to work on a novel, and wished to return to my room as soon as possible.

And I would have done so, but for the drama unfolding before my eyes: a drama that seemed to enact the very script of the book I was working on.

In front of me, I saw the backs of a young British couple, blonde-haired, lean, and outfitted in simple cotton garb in the universal tradition of Yogic Vegetarian World Travelers. The couple had just ordered a vegetarian dinner. Facing them sat a late-twentyish Indian man, mildly chubby-cheeked, drinking a whiskey and water. His dark-complexioned, earnest face, his slightly rakish hairstyle with locks flirting with one side of his forehead, made him look like the typical middle-class Bangalorean scooter-riding gent who spoke Kannada at home and Peter Scot at the local pub. He was light years away from the class of Brown Anglo-Pretenders, who would have thrown him out on his ears had he tried to sneak into a social dance. He was, in other words, a true desi, but merely born to urban parents who had given him an education. This man, this evening, kept talking, and talking, and talking; for this son of the Indian soil, a chap who knew his whiskies as well as his phoren companions knew their daal and their vegetables, had set out to impress the None-but-the-fair who deserve the world (and mostly, get it served to them on a silver platter).

It didn't matter that the couple in front of him, from what I overheard, were a pair of average Britons, moderate achievers, and that he wouldn't have given the time of day to an equal achiever of his own, unmistakably brown skin color. Their pallid epidermis invested them with the magical power to whisk him away from his cursed motherland to a British university, thus rescuing him from this wretched life of his. Their whiteness made them worth impressing. They were the real thing, the Real McCoys.

At first, the Indian tried to impress them with his knowledge in their chosen field as well as in a number of random subjects such as the names of the English local cricket teams. He then began abusing India, bemoaning its poverty of opportunities, which in every case contrasted with the earthly Paradise that was England.

"I am not *contented*. In India, we have too much corruption. English means *quality*," he said, ordering another shot of whiskey, an Indian whiskey named Peter Scot (no relation of Peter England*, the popular Indian clothing line, I believe). [*See Endnote on colonial chic]

He continued, speaking of himself in the second person: "You want to be able to prove your mental ability, but you are not in a position to do it." And then, shifting to the regular person, he told them, "You have social security, but we have *in*security. Anybody can question me. I want *freedom*, you know. These bastards are celebrating 50 years of independence, but the freedom is not there!" These bastards, of course, were his fellow Indians.

"I have merit, but somebody without merit comes and sits here [in my place], because he has a reservation," he continued, echoing the favorite Indian Brahmin complaint against the reservations or job quota system for the lower castes, a "reservations" system that has become a political gimmick and gotten completely out of hand to benefit the wrong people, like the "Women and People of Color" thing in the U.S. "The freedom to choose, to stay as you are — that is not here at all. It is so unfortunate."

Wait a moment! By what rights do I, an expatriate Indian, satirize a younger and greener and less fortunate version of myself? I have the same need and yearning for freedom, after all, and often find myself fighting for it, from whoever I perceive as withholding it from me. Except that I was now *outside* the fish bowl and what I was observing before me was a troubling paradigm of the modern world. What bothered me, and what should disturb all Indians, including those who do likewise, was his act of *complaining to the British* that his fellow Indians had created a less-than-level playing field for him. Fifty years after we had received our independence from the British, at least according to the history books and the official documents, fifty years after the British judges and magistrates and complaint-takers had finally departed, Indians were still going to the British and to other Westerners with complaints about their fellow Indians: wife-beaters, caste-minded bigots, bride burners, and sexists. And all of us were doing it, from this unemployed engineer to Arundhati Roy! It was intolerable![11]

Let me say that I have nothing against the British couple in this incident. It was not their fault that they were white (well, not entirely their fault, anyway, though their parents could have tried to fool around with the help). Indeed, I thought that they behaved

---

[11] I was doing it too; except that I, or my fictional character in *The Revised Kama Sutra*, was saying to the West, "Yes, we Indians are fucked up. But *you* bear the responsibility, you s.o.b.s!"

admirably, stretching their politeness and patience a million times more than your average Texan or New Yorker would have. The only indication that all the lights in their brains, except for those lighting the exit signs, had switched off came from the paucity of their responses, their increasingly frozen manner. But every time they made an attempt to leave, they were foiled by his abject thanks and expression of self-loathing, which embarrassed them into staying a little while longer.

"I am very grateful to you. I asked you for an inch, and you gave me a yard," said the man, as he went on. He explained to me later that he had met the couple at three o'clock that afternoon, followed them around the park, allowed them a short respite (or perhaps they had briefly escaped his clutches), and then reconnected with them and continued his conversation as they ate their typically British pure vegetarian dinner, while he confined himself, like a 100 percent authentic Indian, to a diet composed strictly of cigarettes and booze.

When they once again expressed a desire to leave, he said, "Sure, sure. After all, who am I? I am just a by-passer. I'm just a good-for-nothing bastard. I can only open my mouth and do blah blah blah. I thank you very, very much."

Feeling sorry for him, they stayed on a little longer, watching him down a few more shots of whiskey as he promised them, in a slight shift of mood, that India could, given the opportunity, be the best. "Indians make the best Englishmen, the best Australians, the best Americans, the best Japanese," he declared.

What?! I admit that immigrant Indians are an impressively "integrating," monkeying-around, and even acrobatic bunch, and they probably really do make the best Republicans apart from American WASPs (take Dinesh D'Souza, for example), and the best fakers of English accents apart from the British themselves. I admit, too, that the late Anthony Burgess claimed that some of them were writing better English than the English. But do they really make the best *Japanese?*

Like a true brother of mine ("Hello Brother," the Louis Armstrong song briefly came to mind), he was being carried away by his passion.

He expanded on his rather startling declaration: "If you want to hear good English, you can *only* hear it from an Indian. You can hear good French from an Indian, good Japanese from an Indian — not even from a Japanese." Would Indians, given the chance, the funny diapers, and fifty raw eggs a day, also make the best sumo wrestlers? I wondered.

"When the opportunities are there, India will reign supreme. Want to bet? I will bet it with my life."

To prove his point, he offered not his rather cheap life, but an anecdote. "A 12-year-old Indian became a graduate in the U.S.A. You have not heard it? It was in all the newspapers." He was speaking of the overachieving Ambati family, which Indian newspapers, local as well as expatriate, had trumpeted as yet another demonstration of India's global superiority in the upper story; few non-Indians in any part of the globe had heard of this story, and the few who had must have relegated it to their private library of freak facts.

When it became obvious that his nationalistic prattle was not working, our guzzler of spirits tried the spiritual hook.

"Do you believe in God? I strongly believe in God. In his mercy." Did he really, I wondered. Or was he trying stealthily to get under their radar with a different strategy, hoping to soften their hearts, which might exclaim, in Heavenly unison, "Praise the Lord! We shall carry out His wishes, and bring His Loyal Brown Servant to our own blessed plot of earth, England! Next week. Avaunt!" Perhaps he was revenging himself for the past invasions of hordes of Bible-thumpers marauding through pagan lands such as ours, and giving these Brits a taste of their ancestors' own medicine?

"We get touchy about things. We get sensitive about things," he continued. He added, unaware that he was contradicting himself, "We are very philosophical."

He was trying so hard. He was so, so grateful. It just didn't seem right, didn't seem fair, didn't seem *decent*, that he should be so grateful to them simply because they were being polite and tolerant (and secretly amused) towards a fellow human being. It wasn't that I wasn't open to encounters between different cultures, between my culture and another culture — even if one of those cultures was still with us, having ruled us for two centuries. Gosh, I was all for it, I wanted it myself. I want armfuls of white friends, of yellow friends, black friends . . . I wouldn't even object to an occasional blonde stranger in my bed. All that I asked for in place of what I saw before me was an exchange between equals, for this Indian was heir to a great culture, and the material poverty of some of its people didn't matter. Unfortunately, even in the present "new" world order (with the MasterCard or Visa issued by Indian banks being "Valid only in India, Nepal, and Bhutan"), there is no equality. And contrary to the Indian's claim, we Indians are *not* philosophical enough, we're not un-materialistic enough — and our poverty shames, angers, and humiliates us to no end.

His final humiliation was yet to come. They paid their bills, excused themselves, and left. No phone numbers had been exchanged, no promises made, no future dates set for this international traffic in minds and talent. His day had been an utter waste. His face looked crestfallen and sheepish. He ordered his eighth shot of bottled poison.

And I could not bring myself to detest my fellow-Indian. I understood him, because I had been there. His white objects of desire had abandoned him with barely concealed disgust, but I felt compassion for him. I broke the ice by smiling and saying "Hello." And then I added, solicitously, "Excuse me for saying this, but do you think you should drive home by yourself?"

"Oh, it doesn't matter," he said, crestfallen.

To make him feel better, I asked him what he had thought of his British friends.

He replied, with a touch of sour grapes, "I was not impressed. But they have social life. They are free. We have no freedom. I am sick of it."

Then he asked me where I was from. He must have scented something fishy or not 100 percent local about me.

"Mangalore," I replied, as I often do in such circumstances, not wishing just then to be plied with endless "NRI" ("Non-Resident Indian") questions — how to get American visas and jobs and university admissions, and so on. It was the humble, though not the whole truth; for I could also have said that I was from "New York," having by now spent almost as many years in New York as I had in Mangalore. But the humble truth was simpler, less likely to attract attention.

You could see his face fall so fast, it was a surprise it didn't crash on the floor. He had not the slightest interest in continuing the conversation. After all what could he, a chap from India's Silicon Valley, from the pub-rich, cosmopolitan city of Bangalore, want from some greenhorn hailing from that lousy dump, *Mangalore?*

To have only a few moments earlier been face to face with the white gods, and now to have to submit to humiliating and even condescending questions from the brown resident of a coastal bunghole: it was the ultimate humiliation for the man.

Did a metaphorical tear drop from my eyes, for him, for my country?

Let me come right out and admit it: Perhaps, at some level, and at least in certain fields, such as the game of love, we all have our little con-games, our bag of tricks, and even I have one, though I don't quite know what it is (sometimes, we are unconscious of our deceit, we've imbibed it so early it's become part of our nature). And no one is to blame that some of us are more successful at this con game than others. Besides, who doesn't like success? Who would willingly turn away lights, camera, action, doting women, telephone numbers slipped into your hand or your pockets by aroused women . . . and above all, a life of never having to say "Sorry I stepped on your toe, Mr. Editor" ever again (now, if there is ever a sorry, it will be followed by "do you by any chance have another toe I could step on?")?

I have already made it clear that it is easy to con the Western establishment (provided you follow a good many of the Fourteen

Commandments), and Vikram Seth did it with an bland and insufferably dull novel. So why belabor this point? And yet, the very hugeness of the phenomenon of Arundhati Roy, with her 40 translations and her multi-million dollar fortune, would make this book incomplete without an examination of her success; it would be like writing a history of the ancient world and completely leaving out Greece or Rome.

And let me preface what I am saying is that I am truly excited and hopeful (though with some skepticism at moments) about what she has become in the last one or two years (I, too, share her anti-war leanings). [Added in 2002.] Either she has undergone a tremendous conversion, is on her way to becoming a new Mahatma Gandhi, an uber Mother Teresa, or else she is simply an immeasurably shrewd woman who doesn't need money any more as much as she needs celebrity, attention, and fame.

What made her fortune is her novel *The God of Small Things*, and there are two things to be talked of in this matter: her cute style, and the plot and its elements of violence against women, and incest.

Good writing has nothing to do with bluebottle flies mating, or doing anything else, even though such descriptions may give orgasms to a few spinsters in Idaho. Good writing has to do with honesty, veracity, sincerity, passion, truth . . . not a manufactured truth produced to serve some current literary fashion of incest or some secret international racial program of defaming the colored male. "Her writing has too much yin, it's too writerly, precious, feeding our lack of understanding and our preconceptions of Indian women," said an American woman writer who has been to India, and had the instinct and honesty to realize that Indian women are far more powerful in real life than they are made out to be in the novels that Indian writers feed the cliché-hungry, subjugation-orgasming West.

Around 1996, when she was in the middle of writing her book, Roy had the shrewdness to understand that incest was getting hot, and that "oppressed South Asian women" was a gift something that the world would be grateful for: coming especially, not from a tired old American horse's mouth, but from that of a young Indian filly's.

After all, then that aura of oppressed women could apply to the women of the international baddies too: Iraq, Libya, Saudi Arabia . . . . If it could be established that the Eastern man didn't treat his women right, then it was okay to deny him his rightful place in the world and in the Security Council, to keep him weak by cheating him in international commerce, and to send troops to conquer his country if necessary, killing one hundred colored men for every white man (a pretty fair ratio — what did you expect, that war is fair?). The benefit, if it could be quantified in money terms at all, ran into the hundreds of billions of dollars; and it could be managed for a piddling ten million dollars in public relations money packaged in the form of prizes and "unheard-of royalty advances", which would make the poor brown saps, including such supposed nationalist editors as Vinod Mehta of *Outlook* Magazine grateful to the West indeed. (Of course any unheard-of royalty advances from Western publishers have the automatic effect of making the sheeplike and malleable sections of the West buy a book they have been primed to buy; there's no doubt at all that buzz, especially the buzz surrounding huge advances, makes millions of Western readers go out and buy books. Vikram Seth's according to some readers painfully dull *Suitable Boy* is a brilliant case in point.)

The other remarkable element of Arundhati Roy's novel is the freaks: the freak in the movie theater who sits next to the young boy and makes him masturbate him. Here's the thing: there will always be freaks, in every society on earth. And there may be proportionately a few more in India, because when economists and sociologists measure the health or sickness of various nations of the world, such as deaths per thousand, or average ages, or doctors or income per capita, there is one measurement they completely forget to include, one that affects the basic health of a country: fucks per capita. And by this measurement, Indians are probably the poorest people on earth, and many of the Arab nations which produce terrorists are probably not too far behind (though the wealthy in both societies are never hampered by this statistic, which doesn't apply to them).

The reason we have more freaks in India, probably — and if not for yoga and spiritual diversions, we might have had many more — is that we are so sexually desperate, and so forbidden and unavailable is normal sex for major segments of the population, that it could drive the most starkly heterosexual male to consider a homosexual fling — or, worse, decide to screw his sister.

On the other hand, there is absolutely no proof that domestic violence occurs in a greater percentage of Indian homes than American or British ones — exceptions being the homes of a few poor Christians, alcoholics, and others who are dispossessed and uprooted (slum dwellers), and in the process, degenerated. If Arundhati Roy really cares for suffering persons (and I am beginning to think she does), then she would not bat for the four percent of Indians who engage in incest, say, or the twelve percent who are victims of domestic violence; she would fight to increase the number of fucks-per-capita for the Indian male, who is so pitifully underfucked his penis should get decorations for its no-first-use, no-second-use, and rarely-ever-used policy.

And this is true of married men too. Why not fight against the horror of wives who put their prime part into cold storage right after the last child, and use this prize possession to commit sexual blackmail on their husbands, who are reduced to weakness in most Indian households, especially South Indian ones — North Indian households being the main exceptions?

But then, I suppose, Roy knew that most readers of fiction are white women, and white women don't want to think about brown men with untended erections. They want to think of Tom Cruise or Ben Affleck with a boner, not some brown man in Kerala — unless they can be made to hate the poor fucker.

Some Indians are likely to respond: Come on, why expose someone else's business operation, scheme, or racket? Why not run one of your own? Don't we all have to make a living — isn't this one of our *duties* in life? That's the way some Indians think, but that is not the way I think, having been brought up to think that we are here on earth for some larger purpose, some purpose greater than ourselves. Which is why you couldn't even begin to describe my indignation when the only question one Indian who had just met me had to ask me when I told him I was a writer — he didn't care whether I wrote poetry or pornography, didn't bother to ask — was, "What is the break-even point in *this business*?"

Business! *Business*! I say, *fuck* business! For me, writing has never been a business, but a passion, a passion for expressing myself and of using my talent, such as it is, to fight injustice. It is these elements that I seem to perceive in the recent Arundhati Roy, a much more interesting person in my book now, which gives me the pleasant suspicion that our separate and highly individual dysfunctional Indian Catholic childhoods nevertheless managed to leave in both of us a smidgeon of conscience and of missionary fervor.

THE ROLE OF ETHNIC SHAME IN THE COLONIAL AGENDA

The most important thing is to be whoever you are without shame. — Rod Steiger

If you are an Asian on the run from yourself, from your history and identity, and from your own people — and if your own people run away or avert their eyes the moment they see you approaching — whom can you turn to, whom do you befriend, whom do you walk towards, whom do you depend on for your happiness?

On white people.

Ay, there's the rub. There's the crux of the problem, one of the major reasons why some of us abandon or stop trusting our own people and try to impress the whites.

That is why it will be a freezing day in Madurai before we Indians unite, and stop selling our bottom cherries to the highest white bidder.

I said "Indians"; other colored people will have to look within themselves and see what role ethnic shame, and its most frequent corollary, a deferential awe towards the West and Western civilization, is true of their own impressing-the-whites operation. But it would only seem logical that once you have determined that your salvation depends on white people, you will learn to adapt, to summon up every ounce of your energy, wit, and cunning towards impressing them.

In my limited observation, ethnic shame is a phenomenon that is particularly intense among Indians abroad, and particularly those in the U.S. and U.K. (somewhat more so in the latter), and sometimes more so among those persons of Indian heritage who have migrated to the West from countries in Africa and the Caribbean. And within these groups, the people who suffer from it the most are those who have been subjected to religious conversion and forcibly alienated from their roots: Catholics from India, or Anglicans from the Bahamas, for example. It is far less to be found in countries that have never, or only briefly, been colonized: Japan and Thailand, for example, have very little, and the Chinese, whose colonization was relatively short compared to India's, have it in smaller quantities.

Let me furnish some living comparisons.

In San Francisco's Chinatown, there is a bakery-cum-eatery where old and young Chinese men gather to sip cheap tea, eat pastries and shout, argue, gossip. Every one of them there — every one, with the exception of this crackpot alien who will mingle with the natives in their proletarian greasy spoon with sticky tabletops — every single one of them is Chinese, celebrating their common Chineseness, discussing the old country as well as the new country perhaps, loud and happy to be alive.

But where in the New York-New Jersey area, the heartland of the Indian-American expatriate community, is the Indian equivalent of Delhi's India Coffee House, where men are men and not afraid to show their unapologetic brown faces and proclaim their essence and shout their opinions — Arre, behn chot!?

In no place at all. In almost every public place outside of India — even Indian restaurants — one notices that Indians seem to be ashamed of their Indianness, avoiding reminders in-the-flesh, looking away — gazing at their feet, trying to avoid being pinned down by probing desi eyes, trying to appear oh-so-proper and British ("We haven't been introduced, have we?"), disowning their blood bond with the common denominator Indian who forms the common Westerner's stereotyped experience of an Indian: "Oh, I am not *that* type of Indian." Even in Indian restaurants, the Western customers stride in and out like peacocks, while the Indians slink in and out like guilty, shamefaced, plucked turkeys.

What are they ashamed of? What is our Unspecific Original Shame?

To probe which, let's consider for a minute the coconut-palm-covered southwestern coast of India. Here, in the town of Mangalore, my aunt reported with glee of a fashionable local woman who had received her comeuppance: "She was riding on the pillion of her husband's scooter in Hampankatta with her sari tied so low. And then her sari rode down exposing her bum line. And everybody was laughing at her. And her husband was humiliated, saying: 'My *laz* — my shame or *maryad* — is gone.'"

According to this mind-set, you have only one helping of shame that God gives you when you start your life. Once you lose it, it's gone. You can never get it back again. You might as well commit suicide (and in Hindi movies, suicide is indeed a highly recommended and noble option when a shameful event occurs).

Had this woman been an American, this episode of accidental demi-semi-mooning might have fetched her an appreciative, sap-stimulating whistle or a Kodak moment at most, nothing more — if not a yawn. It certainly wouldn't have been transferred the very next day to the communal history book, to be inscribed there indelibly, forever.

Another reason: While Indians often bewail foreign stereotypes of India, both 60-Minutes-negative and New Age positive — and justly so — Indians themselves, most often, have the most ignorant notions of their own countrymen. Residents of North India, where Christians are numerically insignificant, get their ideas about Indian Christians (a group as varied as the areas and the Europe-like variety of subcultures they come from) from the typically egregious and fantastic Hindi feature films (like *Julie* or *Bobby*) in which Christians have been portrayed as cowards, drunks, and easy lays; whereas the truth is that in general Indian Christians, battered and browbeaten by Victorian and fundamentalist Christian notions of sex as sinful, are far more protective of their virginal treasures than their non-Christian counterparts.

The result of this kind of mistaken categorization — either of your subgroup at the pan-Indian level or of your nation in a non-Indian country — is ethnic shame. To be moved to deny your ethnic background, or to make attempts to cloak it in acquired gestures and cultures as ill-fitting as a cummerbund on the proud belly of a South Pacific island chief or a necktie on that of a Papuan tribal wearing his penis gourd, that is ethnic shame. Ethnic shame is the opposite of ethnic pride and it is a sublime example of how colonialism has managed to co-opt us in our own subversion, and in our alienation from our culture and our earth, and ultimately in the extinction of our own culture.

So when India's former Prime Minister Deve Gowda visits Laos wearing a lungi, the South Indian sarong, Indians are ashamed of him and of themselves; whereas when an African head of state visits India wearing his colorful native costume, Indians applaud him for adhering to his own culture. When Gowda eats with his hands or eats a ragi mudde (a sticky peasant food made of a dark grain called ragi) instead of a cucumber sandwich or crumpets, Indians are again ashamed of their Prime Minister. Why? Because at some level, the British and their missionaries and their educators convinced us, over 200 years of rule, that we are an inferior, uncivilized nation of idol-worshiping savages whose low morals were obvious in such cultural landmarks such as the erotic Khajuraho temples and the "filthy" *Kama Sutra.*

No doubt ethnic shame is a condition that afflicts many Third World societies, and many parts of India, which is why we are so gleeful and proud when a Western cultural authority praises our philosophy or proclaims our "Indian" beauty Miss Universe (*they* said it, after all). But I will admit, for purposes of a more detailed case study, that it is far truer of my own community of Konkani Catholics than it is of, say, Konkani Gowd Saraswaths or Iyengar Brahmins, particularly those of us Konkani Catholics who live virtually alone in alien lands. We try to defend it, this ethnic shame, as representing a cosmopolitan attitude, and it may indeed be true that we're more cosmopolitan and less parochial than certain other Indian groups, but let us admit that at some deep level, we are hobbled by a kind of ethnic shame.

The insufficiency of ethnic pride, while exceptionally acute among Mangalore Catholics, is a general affliction of Indians, when you contrast us for example with the Japanese, who are so steel-spined they have great trouble apologizing for the rape and genocide committed by their parents and grandparents in Korea, China, the Philippines, and other parts of Asia (in fact my father's own story of inhuman treatment at their hands is published in *Eaten by the Japanese: The Memoir of an Unknown Indian Prisoner of War*). In contrast, educated Indians feel that they must apologize for every Indian who spits or shits by the roadside, for India's official corruption, for the poor quality of Indian manufactured goods, for our repeated defeats by foreign conquerors, for our dirt and disease and poverty, now and forever. Faced with such a burden, it is no wonder that some Indians succumb to the temptation of simply denying their Indian origins, just as the well-known *New York Times* book critic, Anatole Broyard, a fair-skinned black of mixed parentage, successfully kept his black origins secret almost till his death. (Why? Why? Why did it matter so much? A question worth asking ourselves honestly, even today!)

Why is ethnic shame such a serious matter, and not just some personal oddity? Because, whether practiced by Indians or Arabs, Filipinos, Sri Lankans, or former *New York Times* book critics, it contributes to our collusion with the forces that tend to make us invisible in a foreign society. The shame of having the wrong color, the wrong religion, the wrong accent, the wrong climate, the wrong clothes, the wrong friends . . . . If you are a Konkani, this shame is compounded by your shame at being marginal in Indian society, of having a language without a script, of not having a great literature, of never having had political power, of always having been ruled. Throwing our hands up in despair, some of us decide to power-wash away our "ethnic" elements, and to blend, almost undetectably, into the Majority White society. But deep inside us, a tiny voice whispers: *You sold out!*

There will be no end to this steady watering down of culture, and of ethnic definition, unless we analyze this shame and its components and figure out ways to deal with it.

One component of ethnic shame is body shame: Until the early decades of this century, many of the local women of South Kanara, like the women of Kerala, used to go around topless, a colorful feast for sore eyes, their natural beauty a match for the lush, green surroundings. There was no two-drink minimum, and no admission charge to this show. It simply was the most sensible way to dress in a climate as hot and muggy as Mangalore's. The Christian influence in Mangalore — more so than the Muslim influence that was so decisive in North India — changed that. Until a few decades back, when Saint Elvis and Saints John, Paul, George, and Ringo followed the glorious trail of Saint Francis and brought the Gospel of modernism and short, tight skirts to Mangalore, young Christian girls wore long-sleeved blouses that covered their wrists and necks, roasting them on hot days. The body had become a thing of shame.

A second component is language shame — the shame of speaking your own language. Which is such a crying shame, because language is what distinguishes us from the rest of the animal world. Language is the basis of culture. If colonialism can make you ashamed of your language, it has won the war. We Konkanis have a mellifluous, flavorful, and rich language, a language full of humor and earthiness, especially in its unsanitized versions — a word like potli, which means package, also refers to a man's genitals, their size and their relative visibility through his clothes — a very funny notion. But the too pious Christians, the upper classes, and the urbanized among us have lost this earthy language with its salty idioms. Partly because if you and I attempt to speak two words of it, some other alienated soul from Mangalore is going to laugh at us, stopping us in our attempts to be free. For example my fellow Konkani friend Ralph, who will laugh at my use of Konkani, and then his, and then confess that a self-hatred of his own disconnection to his culture propels the laughter. Our accent or our vocabulary is not good enough, so we withdraw into further ignorance and further disconnection. Shame and scorn have been ingrained in our natures, making it impossible for us to get out of this trap, which we help make permanent.

* * *

I return now to the basic question posed earlier: What are we Indians so apologetic about that we sometimes deny our Indianness or go out of our way to avoid smiling at or speaking with other Indians in foreign lands? That we come from a culture in which, as in many Asian countries, people wash their behinds instead of using toilet paper like the Westerners? Now that even the President of the world's most powerful country has had to lower his chaddi or underpants for Paula Jones's lawyers to inspect their contents (remember the Distinguishing Characteristic?), I call upon ten prominent Indians led by the Indian Consul-General in New York (I'd like to spare that worthy, the Indian Ambassador, lest he never be invited to sit — yes, *sit*, it's no use trying to lead me astray into misspelling that word — at the American President's table again) to publish a one-page advertisement in the New York Times: YES, WE ARE BUM WASHERS AND PROUD OF IT.

This suggestion proceeds from the premise, espoused by Western Europeans, non-puritan feminists, assorted nudists, and Digambara Jains, that by exposing our "shame," we free ourselves from fear, and free ourselves from being tyrannized by shame — shame about what is natural, what is purely biological, and what is, from an Indian philosophical perspective, mere surface and illusion.

But there are other, more serious reasons for our shame, no doubt: the Western media's and the American people's association of India with highly negative images such as abject poverty and bride-burning (while the former has some merit, the latter is about as fair as associating the United States with cannibalism or London with Jack the Ripper-type mass murders just because of a couple of well-publicized historical incidents and some popular notions whose absurdity people don't want to face). A good example is the belief commonly held by Fat Cat Indian Immigrants who arrived here with medical degrees, family support, or large amounts of monetary backing "that *all* Indian immigrants have it easy in America," and that therefore any Indian who, after ten years of life here, is driving something humbler than a Mercedes has only himself to blame.

But many Indians don't have it easy when they arrive in America. They don't have relatives, jobs prearranged by friends or family, quickly recognized medical degrees, money, the right accents, the confidence of an upper-class Indian past, or the support of immediate family members; such Indians may have to wait months or years to get their visas. Some of us must start from scratch, and the rest of us need to ask: are we being compassionate to those who didn't have it as good as us? Many of us are embarrassed when we see an occasional Indian making a monkey of himself — say, an Indian who walks into a McDonalds and tries unsuccessfully to sell ball point pens to the burger-eaters — and to top it all the man has a bad haircut and ill-fitting pants or perhaps a pink Sikh turban . . . . But why should you feel shame? And why should you think he's making a monkey of himself? He's a man. He probably didn't have your breaks. He's trying to make a living. If that's shameful, or if he is indeed making a monkey of himself . . . well, brown-skinned persons have as much of a right to make monkeys of themselves as persons of any other color. With one billion Indians populating the planet, we have a right to have at least one million representatives from every character type the world has ever known.

It's not an easy public relations job being an Indian, I admit. There are one billion of us, yet when a handful of us desperate ones (and sure, India has desperate people) do things like tearing up our passports on an airplane in order to claim political asylum at the next landing site, nearly every Indian suffers enough by association as to get treated nastily by airline personnel and visa officers the world over. Even other Third World countries like Cuba, who have no particular racial or political reason to dislike India, harass Indians while letting Americans — yes *Americans*, whose government is currently conducting an economic blockade of their country — sail through the immigration line. The India Haters Club is growing larger and larger, and its largest contingent is probably the millions of *Indians* for whom a few bitter experiences of betrayal have pushed them over the edge into self-hatred: *Yes, my skin is brown, but my soul is white.*

And now, children of American Indian parents will tell you they are ashamed of their Indian food (they don't want to take it to school in their lunch boxes), of the awkward manners and "foreign" dress of their parents and grandparents, and also of their country and its poor image — which their partly shame-afflicted parents have failed to project positively.

Maybe it's time that India's leaders, software billionaires, and others studied this issue and underwrote a huge, global public relations campaign, so that other nations, as well as we ourselves, are able to give India, fellow Indians, and the one-sixth Inner Indian within all of us human beings, their proper due. It is an idea whose time as come, as the number of wars and the unhappiness caused by bigotry are increasingly unnecessary in an age in which we are moving closer to a world wherein a man or a woman can say: I am not only a man, I am also partly a woman, and partly an American, and one-third an Asian, and one-sixth an Indian, one-hundredth a Jew, and one-fiftieth an anarchist (and so on — this is just an arbitrary list), because all these tendencies and elements are blended in me. The age of purity, racial or national, is dead — or should be.

IMPRESSING THE REINCARNATED WHITES

"It's about our balls," I finally told a few of the 150 Indians — with a combined net worth of at least one hundred million dollars — who had collectively coughed up a beggarly $400 in response to three passionate, mailed appeals and readings to benefit the Invisible Man Press, which I had conceived as a community effort in publishing, a publishing company designed to give our deepest and most hidden feelings free expression. Of course, why should they have believed me? Just because I said so? But these Indians were supposed to be my *friends*, and at least a few of them knew that I had written a book lauded in India for its outspokenness, its humor, and its rich description of Mangalore and its Catholic community in particular. I had known them for about ten years, had been to their parties, hosted them at my home, met them at common friends' houses, spoken for hours with them, eating their food and drinking their Diet Sprite and talking with their kids. And they had treated me like a total stranger, like a bum who had just walked in from the streets. Most hadn't even had the courtesy to give me a phone call either to express support or to ask questions.

Having not been in touch with other artists, writers, and cultural organizers who have similar experiences about Indian tightfistedness, I was dismayed. It was at the end of that year-long frustrating process that had wasted about two weeks of my time and about two months of my focus, that I uttered the brutal words, "This project isn't a business, isn't about making money, isn't my private project, isn't some motel or new pyramid scheme. *It is about our balls.*"
[Explanation: So long as the American literary establishment dictates

what writers can and cannot write — and your writers are the equivalent of your priests, your prophets, your spokesmen, your historians — they have you by the balls.

So here I was, a solitary activist, a Socrates appealing to their conscience, a missionary for freedom, ringing the bells for the Indian Balls Salvation Army (with the slogan SOB — Save Our Balls), and the Indians or ex-Indians were responding, "Balls? What's that?" (In my restricted Long Island world, I didn't know then that other Indian writers had similarly been rebuffed, that an Indian poet-publisher's customers were almost all white, and that a Mangalore author trying to get support from millionaire Indian doctors for a huge research project had not even covered his travel expenses to their homes.)

In the meantime, the Indian community in America, which collectively earns over $35 billion a year, had collected a million and a half dollars to impress Columbia University, to persuade it to institute a Chair in Indian Studies — to have Columbia's permission, sanction and blessing as it were, to study their own mother country under an American, Columbian flag.

Though my appeal was meant to be addressed only to Indians, one letter had mistakenly reached a white couple on our address list. The response to this accidental appeal to this white couple? 100 percent. They, a retired couple with a per capita income perhaps one-tenth of that of our Physician and Businessman 150 Elite group of friends, came up with $250. They insisted I take it, and convinced me they felt honored to help me. They have also been perhaps the strongest and most uninhibitedly enthusiastic supporters of my writing ambition in the last ten years, beginning even before I received my "validation" as a writer with a Penguin India contract.

Dammit, dammit, dammit. As a result of a stupid, random accident, the whole thesis of this book (whose publication had been delayed for four years because at the crucial time I was discouraged by brown author-columnist Khushwant Singh's disapproving remarks — though Khushwant is a fine person in many ways) — a thesis which my idealistic and wholesome part had desperately been hoping to prove wrong — had been proved resoundingly correct.

The thesis, which was actually Ashok the Buddhic Rough Diamond's thesis — *if you wish to succeed, impress the whites, you fucker!* — had been personally discovered by me after three years of labor and pain. Oh, shoot! I thought Had I concentrated the same energy in soliciting funds from people who were . . . white*, I might have reached my financial goal years before this. Instead, I had *lost* thousands of dollars worth of money, time, energy, and hope. All for a measly $400. In the meanwhile, in a different deal, an Indian had cheated me of $8,000.[12]

As for the balls I was invoking in my appeals: here, too, I was the beneficiary of New Wisdom. You know these mafia conferences between rival families, when everyone attending is supposed to check their weapons in at the door? Most Indian and Asian immigrants have checked their balls in at the door the moment they entered America or Britain. That has been the "price of entry." It is my belief that these balls are collected and fed into a gigantic ball crusher at JFK International Airport, and the juice is recycled either to flavor iced tea (it has always tasted weird to me, I'll never get how others like it), to make the secret ingredient in Coca Cola, or to concoct one of the aphrodisiac preparations sold to men to avert mid-life decline.

So terrified are these ball-less outwardly brown and inwardly New White persons, that an Indian without a Western imprimatur would be treated with more cruelty by them than by the average white liberal. Because the average white liberal doesn't know you, he is at least willing to give you a hearing. Not these coconuts. If you have failed to impress the whites, you are . . . scum! Out! And please don't darken their whitewashed doors again.

One cannot help feel sorry for this Indian habit of measuring oneself according to the verdict of white people. To paraphrase Descartes' famous statement: *They* think of us on occasion; therefore

---

[12] Sorry, so sorry, I promise to be color-blind from January 1, 2001 onwards, but there's simply no way to get around the race factor: even though, idealistically speaking, I would like to run away from them, the facts in this case are black-and-white.

we are. If an Indian-American kid wins a spelling bee in Tuscaloosa, we must trumpet this in our newspapers to make ourselves feel good.

How powerful They have become in our Innermost Sanctums is illustrated by the desperate attempts of a well-meaning friend to get friends and acquaintances to vote in the *Time Magazine* online poll for the 100 Greatest Persons of the Century, so that Mahatma Gandhi, pretty low down in the list at the time, could at least outperform Adolf Hitler. As if their fucking opinion matters, as if their opinion makes or does not make Gandhi one of the 100 Greatest Fucking Persons of the Century.

Indeed, many of these immigrants are so terrified of voices that may offend the Masters that they will themselves act as filtering devices, as local policemen or toughs. Organizations like the Asia Society, South Asian Journalists Association (SAJA), and many ethnic newspapers regularly act as cheerleaders for those Indians who have impressed the whites, and as bouncers to keep their scruffy and impolite brethren from disrupting the harmony, on one occasion trying to drop a "trouble-making" Indian author from the program at the Asia Society. Their invitation lists are directed either to the collection of funds, or to flattering the local white power structure. The organizer of SAJA, described by a friend as the typical "sabha secretary," had in three months in late 1999, bagged three biggies as speakers — Arundhati Roy, Abraham Verghese, and Suneeta Peres da Costa, the most recent hot South Asian babe in a long line of flavor-of-the-month babes to come — and his excited, pubescent hype showed that he was basking in the reflected glory of his white-sanctified celebrities. Did a single one of the hundreds whom he had invited carry the stamp of "Approved by Indians; *Disapproved* of by the White Establishment"? No. The idea was unthinkable. Dissent was un-American, and therefore un-Indian-American. (Whew? Did I really say that? So be it!)

I tried to tell one of these suited-and-booted coconuts: "If you have time and energy and money to spend to encourage art, why spend it on those who are already wealthy and famous from being recognized by the Western establishment? They don't need your pennies, your praise, your garlands, and your long speeches! They scorn you behind your backs as mentally vacant bores and suck-ups! Whereas, to a struggling Indian artist, especially one saying something different, your encouragement could mean the difference between life and death!"

The coconut replied: "But we praise them and honor them not because they *need* our praise. We praise them and honor them because we *want* to!"

It was like talking to a brain that had been made impenetrable with ten coats of Teflon.

And how did a magazine called *The Indian-American*, extremely rare in the Indian-American community for its hospitality to unneutered, unbridled, and virile expression, die out? Because its readers, many of whom were disappointed to learn of its demise, had in large part been relying on and getting complimentary issues. Perhaps some didn't understand that free expression isn't free, that someone, ultimately, has to pay for it, and that if that someone is a big businessman or a corporation, then something extremely valuable is being filtered out or lost in the process of appeasing these sponsors.

Is it possible that after a thousand years of slavery or foreign conquest, we are terrified of freedom, and would crucify those among us who talk about it and fight for it? Afraid that, as a result of our loose speech, or the loose talk of some loose cannons among us, we might be booted out of America, just asked to roll up our beddings, to pack up our sorry tiffin carriers, and vamoose?

The Indian community is one of the most docile in America, and sometimes even trumpets this fact as a virtue whenever it goes a-begging to the whites for favors. No doubt this docility is suitably rewarded and treated as good behavior by the white establishment: *Newsday*, Long Island's monopoly newspaper, ran a two-page feature on a chap named Bobby Kumar, who had endeared himself to the local white establishment for nothing really spectacular except for . . . . . his *talent for being endearing!*

If you are looking for generosity, openness, compassion, don't hope to find it among the reincarnated whites. Go East, young men, back to your own countries, where at least a few thinking souls will be hospitable to your point of view, and the color of your skin doesn't immediately demand an identification document signed by a white authority.

SHAME AND PUBLIC SCHOOLS

Pankaj Mishra's *Butter Chicken in Ludhiana* is a book rich in observation, humor, and humanity, and I greatly enjoyed reading it. There's just one problem that Mishra seems to share with many Indians who have been victims of a highly Anglicized educational system. He bears on his frail shoulders the Sensitive Brown Sahib's Burden: embarrassment and shame at realizing that his fellow Indian males, especially the ones who didn't get schooled in Anglo-Imitative Snob Academies, have *penises*. Consider that but for the deep and scarring influence of Macaulay — indeed, he is the quintessential Macaulay's Child, as all English-speaking Indians are to a greater or lesser degree — he might have been the author of *Buttering Chicks in Ludhiana*.

For, like almost every other *successful* male Indian writer writing in English these days and receiving some Western recognition, or the recognition of Western proxies in India, he is a public school product — meaning, the product of an expensive and exclusive privately run school modeled on English "public schools" such as Eton, Harrow, and Rugby. Consider that in a country with over twenty thousand high schools and colleges, the graduates of three exclusive Indian public schools and three colleges — the McOxbridges of India, which often send their graduates on to the real Oxbridges and their American counterparts — in three Indian metropolises account for more than half the published and ballyhooed literature written in English. While Rushdie attended the original article, Eton, in Mother Britannia, Vikram Seth, Amitav Ghosh, and others are alumni of the top Indian public schools; Seth, Ghosh, and Arundhati Roy were personally known to each other in Delhi long before they became stars. What a coincidence, indeed! Truly a small world. And it is this small circle that is projected by the Western media to Western readers as *the* India.

With the partial exception of Roy, who broke the barrier, and the bank, with a little incestuous suggestiveness and exposed sex organs (in her prose) at just the politically correct time, when the Western public appetite craved a little Indian female exhibitionism, all of these public school writers suffer acutely from the disease of Subcontinental Shame, more specifically penis shame.[13] Could there be a connection here? Could these public schools be "shame academies"? Rushdie, who derides Pakistan and India for their concept of shame, seems to me to be, like most public school products, also a prisoner of a kind of shame: the fear of ridicule, which appears to be, secretly, one of the most powerful influences on the behavior of many Indians who are psychologically Anglo-Indian.

Could any of these writers stand totally naked before the world, having written a daring and unzipped novel? Not even if they were paid good money to. Shame would intercept the words and choke them before they were out of their speakers' throats. Salman Rushdie, as an American writer observed, could never write a novel in which the central male character sharing some characteristics with himself can be ridiculed.

Why do these public schools produce such personable yet shame-schooled products? I've asked myself. Along with the debates, the Anglophilia, the blazers, the insignia, and the neckties, could it also be the dehumanizing practice of ragging, which in extreme forms, might sap the will to be an individual, standing alone against the system?

An insurance policy against such tendencies might be for

---

[13] Explained and illustrated at length in my novel *The Revised Kama* Sutra, where it is defined as "a psychological affliction, occurring mostly in the Third World, and especially former British colonies, in which males of the "age of reason" feel ashamed of their penises, and make every possible attempt to hide their defining organ's existence from fellow human beings."

nonwhite countries (especially the public schools within them) to teach their students to love and cherish their own and other Eastern cultures. To think that I was able to pass out of a not bad Indian school and college, winning a university rank and a gold medal to boot, without acquiring the rudiments of my own ancient culture, being so illiterate about my own culture's major (Hindu) myths that I could not even write an informed ten-page essay on Indian culture — it is a scandal! The idea that the school has no responsibility for teaching culture, that culture is an optional acquisition while "knowledge" or rote-learning is not, is a nefarious idea, with roots in the British design for the creation of robotlike, Brit-friendly baboos or clerks meant to serve, compute, and keep the records of the Raj, but not to think.

Also regrettable is the white-impressing racism of India's academic curriculum, which admits no James Baldwins, no Richard Wrights, no Ralph Ellisons, no American slave narratives, no consciousness-arousing black writers. A recent *India Today* article neutrally comments on how the modern urban young have "attitude," which they demonstrate — the article goes on to explain — by wearing a particular shade of lipstick or low-slung trousers that flash their bum-lines (their Vedic ancestors would be very, very proud, having flashed far more than their bum lines in the open fields while performing an important 64-part ritual). Given the pervasiveness of American culture in the media, our curriculum needs to incorporate an Anti-American-Dream corrective, including books by modern Indian writers who do *not* sing hosannas to Western culture — and, yes, of course, James Baldwin, whose *The Fire Next Time* should be read by them until they have passages from it burned in their memory, particularly the one in which he says, "The only thing white people have that black people need, or should want, is power — and no one holds power forever. White people cannot, in the generality, be taken as models of how to live."

And above all, let us know our fellow Indians and our fellow Asians and Third World countries. For example, the persistent myths about Indian Christians have them wearing skirts or shorts and speaking English, whereas millions of small-town Christians can barely speak English, let alone execute a foxtrot, and would never wear a skirt once past school age. When we believe ignorant stereotypes about each other, we can hardly blame Westerners for not knowing better.

But the main theme of this chapter is the shame engendered by a few public schools, whose products in turn dominate the rest of India. How does one presume to be able to affect a change of heart in a system so entrenched and as powerful as that? I am not sure I know the answer, but permit me to throw out a couple of suggestions anyway:

One: Every one of the public school students, before they graduate, should have spent at least 20 days of their holidays living as the guests of middle-class and lower-middle class families, with at least five days being spent in the villages of their schools' low-level staff. And during this time, they ought to eat with their hands, and occasionally help with the dishes.

Two: Let every one of them be made to write on the blackboard one hundred times, once every month. "Yes, I have a dingdong. Yes, I have a pecker. Yes, I possess a penis." Women may be excused from this exercise on "conscientious objector" grounds.

Three: The chief lesson that these schools teach, apart from the minor lessons detailed above? How to Be a Snob, How to be a Brown Sahib, How to Sneer At the Middle Classes and Keep Them in Their Place (i.e. under your heels). No wonder that if you ever find true compassion for the poor in the novels produced by public school graduates, it has probably resulted from a remarkably cunning faking of emotion in the service of the edification of Western consumers. Therefore, it is imperative that international publishers search out and publish non-public-school writers, and that Indian newspapers and other media consciously promote and reserve a few positions at the top for non-public-school graduates, lest the tyranny of Anglo-snobbery, a legacy of the British, continues to choke the voice of the lower classes.

PART III: BLACK? GET IN BACK!

I was reading one of the carefully put together exercises *The New Yorker* publishes constantly as high poetic art, and . . . I was crying because I realized that I could never write like that writer. Not that I had any real desire to, but I knew that even if I had the desire I could not do it. I realized that there was something in me so out, so unconnected with what this writer was and what that magazine was that what was in me that wanted to come out as poetry would never come out like that and be my poetry.
— Amiri Baraka: The Autobiography of Leroi Jones

Each of us, helplessly and forever, contains the other — male in female, female in male, white in black, and black in white. We are part of each other. Many of my countrymen appear to find this fact exceedingly inconvenient and even unfair, and so, very often, do I. But none of us can do anything about it.
— James Baldwin, *The Price of the Ticket.*

DIVIDED, WE'RE SCREWED

In 1980, a year after I joined an American university, when America seemed to be obsessed only by the American hostages in Tehran, I visited Los Angeles and did a typically tourist thing: I took in a show at a standup comedy club called The Comedy Store on Sunset Boulevard. It so happened that Robin Williams dropped in unannounced and gave a hyper-kinetically brilliant performance. In the lineup was a black comedian, who, perhaps short of material, searched the faces in the crowd for a victim, latched on to mine, and hissed, "You're an Eye-ranian, aren't you?" He followed his question with an immediate expletive: "Asshole!" His abuse was so violent and unexpected that I responded with stunned silence. And, though psychologists will describe this phenomenon as perfectly understandable, I am always saddened when America goes on its periodic, xenophobic rages against some foreign, colored country that "will not play ball" and thus earn itself the wagging finger of news anchors such as Ted Koppel. I find it even sadder that black Americans, despite being the primary victims of American racism, will sometimes join in the racist taunting and pillorying of innocents, as during the Iraq war, of people whose only crime was that they "looked" Middle-Eastern. By doing this, they earn their "patriotism" badge, and thus raise their status in the white world by one tiny inch.

Which is sad, because nothing makes it easier for the white races to exercise mental and economic dominance of the world than the racism of colored people towards other colored people. United we have a chance; divided, we're screwed. In certain East Asian countries, Indians and colored people are not welcomed in some places where whites are. A person of Indian origin who says he is an "American" by citizenship is sometimes told no, he couldn't be American, he is probably Arab or Indian. But once they accept his "Americanness," he immediately receives an upgrade in his humanity, his status, and his treatment, with words such as, "Oh, America! Americans good!"

In the oil-producing countries of the Middle East, Arabs have been known to ruthlessly exploit Indians, Thais, and Srilankans, while paying Britons and Americans five to ten times as much for doing the exact same job. Why do the Arabs, who are targets of racism in America and Britain, perpetrate the very racism they ought to oppose?

How has this state of affairs come to pass? Not only the region's own history of colonialism, in which white people have won almost all the major wars in the last two centuries, but their addiction to CNN and American television dramas, in which the Americans are always the good guys (or occasionally, the ones committing an innocent, well-meaning mistake), while others, mostly colored men with funny headgear, are the bad guys.

The most fertile ground for the continuance of racial injustice is in societies wherein the white establishment divides its colored "subjects" into groups, meting out differential treatment to the various subgroups, causing these subgroups to war against each other.

But sadly, there is precious little dialogue between the various nonwhite communities on how to prevent this division. For example, despite the close bonds there ought to be between Indians and African-Americans due to Martin Luther King's debt to Mahatma Gandhi, and the similar freedom struggle experienced by both, there are almost no meetings between African-American community leaders and the Indian community leaders in the U.S., with few leaders trying to overcome the climate of mutual ignorance and stereotyping. In both cases, they're too busy trying to win the favors of the light-skinned.

Racism is racism, but if you must categorize or give labels, then, in

addition to the Dominant Racism of whites towards nonwhites
("dominant" because it is accompanied by powerful, global
consequences for a majority of human beings), there's Reverse
Racism (blacks towards whites), and transverse or Perverse Racism:
Black on Brown, Brown on Black, Brown on yellow, and sometimes,
of Reincarnated ex-brown Whites towards Ordinary Browns. Since
this book takes a universal approach, one must not forget the racism,
in America, of Korean and Japanese immigrants towards other
colored people, including African-Americans. While some of this
racism is inherited from our ancient tribal history and its needs for
self-protection, the ideals we profess today (democracy, equality of
opportunity, the brotherhood of men, the common citizenship and
stewardship of a frail planet and its resources) require that we actively
counter the resurfacing of these tendencies.

One possible strategy: Read writers from other cultures. By
reading passionate writers of different races — honest writers who
are not trying to impress you, or those who will not hold back the
unpleasant truth even if they do try to impress you just a bit with
their language, their decency, or their humanity — you might begin
to transcend your racial myopia and connect with the humanity of
other people. For it is quite likely that if, instead of reading your
seventh Robert Ludlum thriller, you were to devote the time saved to
reading your first-ever novel by an Indian or Chinese or Japanese
author, your mind, your world, and your heart would expand
significantly. To my fellow colored readers, who detect racist strains
in themselves, and to those who wish to understand "what it means
to be an American Negro, and this is who he is — a kidnapped
pagan, who was sold like an animal and treated like one, who was
once defined by the American Constitution as 'three-fifths' of a man"
(James Baldwin), I recommend at least five of the following authors
or books (an incomplete list reflecting my own limited reading):

James Baldwin: The Fire Next Time
James Baldwin: Notes of a Native Son
Richard Wright: *Native Son*

Richard Wright: *Black Boy*
Eldridge Cleaver: *Soul on Ice*
Ralph Ellison: *Invisible Man*
Henry Louis Gates Jr., Thirteen Ways of Looking at a Black Man
W.E.B. Du Bois: The Souls of Black Folk

Indians emigrating to the U.S. with medical degrees that guarantee them a stairway to the top levels of American society often behave as if the credit is entirely theirs, that they don't owe anybody anything. They are fond of taking the line that black people have only their own laziness to blame for their economic backwardness. If so, they need to learn how black civil rights leaders helped bring America to its present state of relative tolerance. They need to hear the words of the wise person who said, "We all owe somebody else. We don't just arrive."

Not only do colored immigrants owe African-Americans for the work they did in resisting slavery and discrimination, but we also have experiences and strategies to share. I remember sharing my chapters on "Impressing the Whites" and "The Fourteen Commandments" with a black man on a flight from Portland, Oregon, to New York's JFK. This man, tall, strapping, and muscular, who had been somber and even intimidating (it seemed to me) through most of the flight, burst out in belly laughs almost twice a minute for the next fifteen minutes as he read through these two chapters. He then said to me, "I grew up in Portland, destined for jail and poverty. And I had to follow almost all of these Twelve Commandments to escape this destiny." It was a moving reminder of how much blacks and Asians had in common despite our differences in history and heritage.

Another anecdote: A black man in a mixed suburb of Long Island reports that he always wears a tie whenever he hangs around in his own backyard on a summer day.

Why, oh why, my friend asks him.

Because, says the man, because the white local police, passing by and seeing him in the yard, might otherwise suspect from his face and color that he was a burglar, and stop to investigate. When on the street, he says, he is always overdressed, wearing an impeccably chosen and ironed suit, because in America you can never say for sure at what point your color or your race might work against you . . . even to the extreme extent of depriving you of your life.

This was this man's burden then, living in his own country, a country his ancestors had given their lives and their freedom to build: to impress the police, or the white people on whom his life ultimately depended, that he was not a criminal; that he was "safe," meaning not a threat; that he could be trusted to walk their streets and not mug an old gentleman or rape a genteel white lady.

He could have said, like James Baldwin, "Well, I know how power works, it has worked on me, and if I didn't know how power worked, I would be dead." And then, "There was something which all black men held in common . . . their precarious, their unutterably painful relations to the white world."

Amen. Unless we have used a little memory whiteout. Let us share in this man's pain, in his humiliation, and his grace. Let us remember that the Western world's message is: "If you're white, you're all right (unless you're a hillbilly or white trash or a poor convicted felon); if you're brown, you don't count, but stick around and look up my behind and check it for warts, Doc, and no bloody snake tricks, please; if you're black, get in back or into jail, unless you're a celebrity or sports star."

The discrimination of the colored towards the colored is also visible in Third World countries. For example, the first thing they ask you in many Muslim countries, even before they have discovered your name or been properly introduced, is whether you are Muslim. If you say you are not, that is held like a grudge against you. In many Persian Gulf countries, a white skin can earn you a salary up to five times as much as an Indian might for doing precisely the same job. White people may even move more freely in such countries.

Also, we Third World countries only learn about each other thanks to Western media, and The West is a cultural dictatorship run by a Board of Fuhrers. They decide who will be important, who will not. From Bali to Bangkok, from Zaire to Zimbabwe, Nobel Prizewinner Amartya Sen is India, and India is Amartya Sen — no other Indians exist, or will, unless the West has brought them to their attention.

The desire for whiteness seems to feature even in certain Southeast Asian countries, where whitening creams are a big item on the store shelves, and many women hope to be fertilized by Caucasian sperm so that the resulting babies are whiter; their social status skyrockets if their babies are fairer, and plummets if their babies are darker. I ran into a few children of Indian fathers and Thai mothers; they seemed to be somewhat apologetic about their dark skin and its darker history. And there is a hilarious story, told in the novel *Bali Moon* (by an Australian author who actually married a Balinese man and experienced Balinese society for over ten years) of a Bali man who discovered that his wife had been fooling around: because her baby emerged from her womb a healthy pink. He kicked out the wife for her infidelity, but kept the baby — whom he proudly named Ketut Tourist. As in George Orwell's *Animal Farm,* where all animals are equal, but some are more equal than others, all sperm are white, but some are whiter than others.

And finally, even India practices colored-to-colored discrimination, which makes it difficult for Indians to be in a position to preach to others. On an Air India flight that was passing through India, I met a Dutch citizen of Indian origin whose ancestors had emigrated to Surinam, enabling him to choose Dutch citizenship. He remarked that the Air India crew treated foreigners and nonresident Indians better than they treated *Indian* Indians. "It's sad to see how they treat the local Indians who board at Calcutta," he said. The message was that even your own countrymen would treat you better if you go abroad and acquire a white veneer.

Depressing, because the converse is never true: for example, no American will be treated better by his countrymen simply and solely because he has visited India or lived there.

And then, I realized that I myself had spent more than an hour conversing with my Dutch co-passenger only after I had discovered his Dutch citizenship.

The poison is lodged deep within us.

It is time to reflect on this: Ever wonder how a mere 5000 Englishmen ruled and subjugated 300 million Indians for nearly 200 years? Because, as the British and other conquerors discovered to their delight: the greatest enemies of Indians are: other Indians. The ranks of the policemen and armies the British used to control Indians came from: India. When a lone Indian rebels against the establishment (or in the modern post-"independence" world, writes satire), there are ten million sad brown fuckers willing to appear from out of nowhere, and for no pay at all, crush that lone Indian.

ROY, RUSHDIE, AND SETH: SPOKESPERSONS[14]

She was petite, she carried a schoolgirl's backpack, she had sultry bedroom eyes, and her conversation had this "Who, me? I'm just this girl in jeans" manner of self-deprecation. Arundhati Roy, entering a packed room at a Bangalore bookstore one glorious evening almost had me falling in love with her. Me, and thousands of others, I am sure. So, if you were Roy-ally seduced into taking temporary leave of your reason or your objectivity, don't be ashamed, and do not feel defensive. Many of us, men, are in love, or have been (love is all we need); many of us women are also in love with a fleeting, wistful "On her throne but for the blasted ungraciousness of God reign I."

I have to admit that I greeted each one of our three West-appointed literary kings or queens — Roy, Salman Rushdie, and Vikram Seth — with an enthusiastic admiration. And for some of the wrong reasons: everybody loves a winner; they had brought some attention — the attention of the *Master* of the Universe — to Indian writing, and to poor, insecure, brown, once-wretched India. (About the same reasons why Indians enthusiastically embrace their beauty queens when they receive international crowns.)

In all three cases, a cooler, more skeptical, more analytical stance, gradually supplanted my earlier uncritical enthusiasm. What changed? It would be dishonest not to admit that in each case, a mild *perceived* slight, a completely trivial action or inaction by the mahatmas in

---

[14] My choice of using these authors as examples, rather than any others, is precisely that because they are so celebrated, and because it is my policy to try to compensate for the tendency of many Indian journalists and academics to suck up to the powerful while trampling on the powerless.

question — or rather, a *perceived* lack of graciousness and generosity by those blessed by fortune and power — had "opened" my eyes. In Rushdie's case, this was a perceived refusal to reply to my two letters, which may simply never have made it past his mountains of fan mail. In Arundhati Roy's case, she, though admitting that she knew who I was (my novel had been talked about on Indian national television and nearly every major Indian English newspaper and magazine about the time she was just starting her first novel), placed a calling card I gave her on the table, turned around, and walked away (absentmindedness, most likely). In Seth's case, it was a case of his abruptly turning his back on me fifteen seconds after I had introduced myself to him, in New York in mid-1993, as a Penguin author with a common friend and editor, David Davidar (he may have been tired, but he had spent at least ten minutes speaking to a white matron just before I, one of the two or three brown writers in the entire gathering, had approached him).

All completely trivial incidents without any significance, because authors are free to choose their own company, and the "niceness" of an author usually has no bearing on the quality of his writing (very often, the greatest geniuses are not necessarily "nice" human beings). I mention these incidents only to be totally candid about any feelings of resentment, and to still claim my right to express my critical opinions. Because, in fact, these incidents were serendipitous for the purpose of this book. *For I do not believe I can be a cool and fair judge of people who I am in love with, or of whom I am an uncritical admirer.* And I don't mean to single these authors out: their behavior, if it was theirs, was only typical of many successful authors, who switch on the floodlights of their charisma for their fans, while directing the flame-throwers of hostility and petty meanness at fellow professionals they *believe* to be slightly beneath them. An example is Rushdie's reported zinger to Vikram Seth, after the latter's tumescent success with the massive *A Suitable Boy*, "I hear you've written a book."

Such behavior is even more flagrant when the competitor is perceived as being far less powerful and as unable to strike back. (Meaning: the weaker competitor has no *white* godfathers, and can therefore be dismissed like a superfluous coolie.) A Bangalore woman writer who approached another female writer who had been famous for only fifteen days told me that the latter refused to divulge the name of her British agent. Still another recent author confessed that when he was writing his first novel, I had been the only one of the many Indian authors he had approached who had been encouraging to him. I guess I felt that it cost me nothing to be gracious, for he posed no threat to me. Though mine is a minority view, I feel we're all unique (or should be) and that there's room enough in the world for all of us (or should be, if things were fairer).

Please don't get me wrong; I do not expect authors to be saints, and I am far from being one myself. In fact, though I think, Rodney King-like, that we should all get along (preferably without being battered into such wisdom), I am grateful to anyone who helps me think clearly, even if it is with an unconscious or absentminded act of discourtesy or unnecessary competitiveness.

However, in *Thirteen Ways of Looking at a Black Man* by Harvard professor and author Henry Louis Gates Jr., American black intellectual Albert Murray is quoted as giving a more sophisticated explanation of this behavior, one that goes beyond mere competitiveness and one that challenges my "there's room enough for us all" theory. Murray says of his more successful friend Ralph Ellison: "Here's a guy who figures that he's got *his* white folks over here, and he got them all hoodwinked, so he don't want anybody coming in messing things up." Henry Louis Gates comments that Murray is seeing the matter "in almost anthropological terms, as falling into the behavior patterns of out-group representatives amid an in-group . . . in anthropological terms, the native informant never relishes competition."

The brilliant Albert Murray and Henry Louis Gates are of course being quite brutal. "Native informant" would be too harsh a term to describe Rushdie, Roy, or Seth; but would it not be correct to describe them as spokespersons, sometimes self-appointed spokespersons for India, highly paid spokespersons who must at any cost prevent fellow Indians from "coming in messing things up" for them? For India, after all, is really much tinier than even Cuba in the Western consciousness, and how many Indian spokespersons can they really handle given that they must also give some air time to white-skinned spokespersons for India such as *60 [Bride-Burning] Minutes* and the former BBC India correspondent and Delhi-resident British-expat "India expert" Mark Tully?

It is worth observing, however, that these spokespersons are not always fully in charge, not always independent actors. They are also products, shrewd and self-aware products of market forces, serving their marketers as well as themselves. Jesse Jackson, admittedly far from perfect as recent stories seem to show, does make a rather insightful observation that Henry Louis Gates Jr. quotes in *Thirteen Ways of Looking at a Black Man.* He says of the phenomenon of General Colin Powell's meteoric rise to near-Presidential candidate: "Historically, there's been this search — whites always want to create *the black of their choice* [italics mine] as our leader. So for the white people this nice, clean-cut black military guy becomes something really worth selling and promoting. But have we ever seen him on a picket line? Is he for unions? Or for civil rights? Or for *anything?*"

This was what some Western publishing reports had said about the new trend in publishing, in which authors such as Arundhati Roy and Chitra Divakaruni are selected not just for their writing but for their looks as well, which must be "something really worth selling and promoting" (to quote Jesse Jackson again).

Again, in the same book, Bruce Llewellyn, a cousin of Colin Powell's, remarks that Powell's story of the poor West Indian kid becoming Chairman of Joint Chiefs of Staff *makes white people feel good.* "They all love this shit. They all love the idea that 'Gee, we weren't prejudiced. A good man came, and we gave him his shot.' White people love to believe they're fair. One of the things that upsets the living shit out of them is when you confront them with the fact that they are really a bunch of racist, no-good motherfuckers." How noble and righteous the Arundhati Roy story must have made Westerners feel: unknown Delhi aerobics instructor picked to become World Author, spokesperson for the Battered/Oppressed Asian/Eastern

Woman, a star drooling with gratitude for the *white* agent who took an eleven-hour airplane trip to the dangerous Wild Eastern tropics, infested with tigers and snakes, just to find her and promote her. Conversely, could we logically assume that it would "upset the living shit out of them" to read an Indian novel which starts with an attack on Western literary apartheid?

It cannot be purely coincidental that many of our West-anointed authors hail from powerful, upper-class Indian families. Life has been good to them, and so has the West, and apart from Rushdie to some extent (in his *Imaginary Homelands* essay "The New Empire Within Britain"[15]), they do not show real anger at the West for having manipulated their people, or any real attempt to stray outside the roles assigned to them. Even Salman Rushdie can be quite accurately described as an astute *player* who has mellowed in his challenges to the Western establishment as he moves closer to Nobel knighthood.

Even if this observation were true, one cannot blame them, for as I have discovered, WWB (Writing While Brown) is almost as dangerous as the offence that black Americans know as DWB (Driving While Black). Of course I mean by WWB: Writing *Brownly* While Brown; coconut-like writing is not in any danger, but on the contrary, is thriving, as Dinesh D'Souza has almost unconsciously discovered.

And if, after achieving a Western imprimatur, some Indian writers begin to distance themselves from fellow Indians (many were distanced by their upper class origins to begin with), or at least from fellow Indian writers, an explanation for it may be found in Anatole Broyard's 1950 *Commentary* essay, "Portrait of the Inauthentic Negro":

> The inauthentic Negro is not only estranged from whites — he is also estranged from his own group and from himself. Since his companions are a mirror in which he sees himself as ugly, he must reject them.

---

[15] The essay is unfortunately dated 1982. As we all know, much water has been passed from the bridge since then. Will the new Rushdie please speak up?

Let the reader judge whether this comment applies in the least degree to our top Indian authors. I am reminded of that famous *New Yorker* photograph of a dozen or so "celebrity" or white-anointed Indian authors flown in from all corners of the world for a group photograph, and the photographer commenting that these subjects seemed very uncomfortable in each others' presence, and had to force themselves to smile for the camera. I, certainly, would prefer to see a lot more true fellowship among Indian writers and Third World writers (perhaps a couple of airplane trips taken at WIPRO's or *The Times of India*'s expense?) incorporating a real conviction that there is room enough for all of us, and competing for the attention of whites is not the only course open to us.

In the spirit of Walt Whitman's All-soul, let me admit that I could be any one of these authors myself, and have indeed been designated a spokesman too, if only by an *Indian Express* headline. This distinguished Indian newspaper granted me a sobriquet of gargantuan scope, one that should make Salman Rushdie jealous, if he values his manhood at all: *Spokesman for the Male Libido.*

WHAT TO DO, BHAI?[16]

Could a slow genetic mutation be compelling nonwhites in scattered parts of the world to prostrate themselves before white people, as the Aztecs did before the conquering Spaniards, though in their case it may have been a mythological coincidence. How else does one explain the phenomenon of Santals and other dark-skinned Indian tribals, living in a world a million times removed from Italian-born Indian prime minister hopeful Sonia Gandhi's glittering Quatrocci Diamond one turning up in hordes to heed her cattle call, to worship at her vacuous shrine?

If it had been merely that success in this life demands that nonwhites attempt to impress the world's most talented, who through an accident of circumstances and some genetic favoritism by the Creator happen to be nearly all white, that might not be such a distressing phenomenon. Instead, we nonwhites unthinkingly prostrate ourselves and make monkeys of ourselves, selling our motherland and our kids in the bazaar, knifing our compatriots in the back, and diluting our culture to please the white gods and goddesses who rule the Earth by divine decree, usually through remote control, but occasionally by marrying into brown dynasties. Millions of us stand and wait to be picked up by the white gods. "Me, me, me, me! Look here! Look at me and help me! And take me with you!" we scream, like a horde of starving refugees on a Rwandan plain, scrambling for the food packages thrown by those cozy, fat do-gooders on a helicopter-borne mission of mercy.

---

[16] Indian English for "What Is To Be Done, Brother?"

This mentality is echoed in my novel, where the main character, not self-aware as yet, writes to Jackie Kennedy, beseeching her to take him to America, where he will gratefully serve as her butler. It is an uncomfortable passage, even for me, but who would deny that at some level, whether more or less sophisticated, it reflects the truth of many of our colored fellow men?

Correcting this undignified state of affairs and changing our habit of mental subservience will not be easy, if at all possible. It must start with the building of a consensus among the Impressors that "impressing" is a craven, shameful disease that all of us must stop simultaneously, because a few lonely abstainers are not going to make a difference. And though I am no guru, being, despite a few lucky breaks, a frail sinner like the next guy — indeed, most of my wisdom, such as it is, has been acquired by the making of foolish mistakes, followed by more foolish mistakes — I will start the discussion ball rolling with a few random ideas or suggestions that are guaranteed 100 percent white-free. In other words, the chief merit of these suggestions (a rare merit these days) is that none of these suggestions have been approved by whites, or written for their approval.[17] Let's call them the ex-Coconut's Bible, then. And I take courage from James Baldwin's words: "I know that what I am asking is impossible. But in our time, as in every time, the impossible is the least that one can demand — and one is, after all, emboldened by the spectacle of human history in general, and American Negro history in particular, for it testifies to nothing less than the perpetual achievement of the impossible."

---

[17] A telling footnote: after I read a section of this manuscript to a very good Indian friend, he suggested I read an Indian author, Ashish Nandy. He then added as an endorsement, unconscious of its irony, "He's very well regarded in the West!" Without having actually seen the book, Nandy's Western reputation, for the purposes of this book, was an anti-endorsement. Then I glanced through a book of Ashish Nandy's, found him fertile and deep, but for the most part writing in a language so convoluted you needed a PhD. to grasp it. Inaccessible to the majority, like Hegel, but unlike Nietzsche, Einstein, or Russell in their generalist writings. I decided to let Ashish Nandy be Ashish Nandy, while I would be myself.

First of all, we need to establish an Eastern Nobel Prize in as many categories as the Western Nobel. Now that Indian billionaires have arrived on the scene, joining dozens of Hong Kong and Japanese billionaires and even a Thai billionaire who also happens to be the country's Prime Minister, let them race to be the first to establish one or more Eastern Nobel prizes (or a rotating Eastern Nobel Prize: given one year by an Indian billionaire, the next year by a Japanese billionaire, and so on) that pay at least 25 percent more in prize money than the Western Nobel. And let this Nobel evaluate the independence and courage of the writer concerned as important criteria in awarding the prize. I also call upon Salman Rushdie to withdraw his candidacy from the Western Nobel by symbolically including a barrage of "dirty words" in his next novel, perhaps calling the Nobel judges dirty names to be doubly certain of being rejected, and then to call up a list of Asian billionaires himself (after all, he is the most famous writer in history, and there is no billionaire or prime minister, except perhaps an Iranian one, who will not return his call) and work towards establishing the Eastern Nobel Prizes — for which he would *not* be considered ineligible, but rather, a prime candidate.

My second suggestion: To discourage the demeaning phenomenon in which We (the Colored) wait for Them (the White Powers) to select us, to take airplane trips from faraway lands and thus to transform our lives, we will have to willingly and generously choose more of our own. We (Indians and other non-Japanese Asian and African countries) are mesmerized by our poverty consciousness, which is an old and outdated habit, even an automatic reflex. We are not that poor; the twelve million expatriate Indians alone are probably worth anywhere from half a trillion to a trillion dollars, and they could easily establish twenty publishing firms the size of Farrar Straus & Giroux, ten each in London and New York — firms that would launch strong, nonconformist, and truth-speaking Indian and Third World writers. One of our Indian billionaires alone could create a couple, greatly adding to his prestige, but with virtually no financial downside that his accountants wouldn't welcome as a much-needed tax write-off — and quite probably, even a slight profit. Of course, the percentage returns may not be as high as for motels, grocery stores, or depressed real estate. But, please, percentages are not everything!

Third: I speak now as a Catholic by birth, and welcome similar soul-searching from other communities, which I do not wish to speak for. With full respect for religious freedom, I suggest that Indian and other Asian Catholics secede from the Church of Rome. Because even if the White Pope were to admit a few brown saints into the Catholic pantheon at this late date, these saints will be tainted, because they have been appointed by whites — and probably as a condescending gesture to political correctness. Be Catholic by all means, if you must, but by direct relationship to your God, not through the favors and beneficence of a coterie of White Intermediaries: for the disease of white-worship in the Indian Catholic community arises partly from its clerical leadership's deference to Roman superiors. Disregard this suggestion only if the Church immediately appoints a colored Pope, and not just a colored Pope, but one who has never in his entire career demeaned himself before white people.

Fourth: When you discover a pattern of automatic and unconscious behavior in yourself, you can only decrease its incidence by watching out for it and then acting opposite to your normal instincts, thus gradually neutralizing the tendency. For example, suppose you are an educated Indian who commonly speaks in English and reads English-language books. If you can find room in your budget for ten books a year by Indian authors (and you really should, if you even half-believe Voltaire's declaration that "books rule the world," and that our inability to write freely keeps us weak), then, determine to purchase at least five books which have *not* impressed the whites to any degree. The principle should not be difficult to understand. When Mahatma Gandhi suggested that Indians buy Indian-made handloom cloth rather than British textiles, he was not making a qualitative comparison; he was not talking about style or durability. He was making a moral argument about the mental colonization — as well as about the destruction of indigenous talent, creativity, and confidence — which were the price of the habit of buying foreign goods.

What if you were one of the 200,000 or so Indians, or perhaps five million Westerners, who have bought only two books by Indians in the last five years: one by Arundhati Roy, and one by either Salman Rushdie or Vikram Seth? It is morally imperative that you go to a bookstore within the next month or so and buy two books by Indian authors who have *not* impressed the whites.

If you desire more scientific countermeasures, make a list of twenty authors, assigning your own value to the absolute merit of their books. For example, you might assign 98 of 100 points for Goddess Arundhati (I'm too scared to give her less), 42 for Kamala Das, and 40 for Kiran Nagarkar (homeboy Indian authors without the polish to get promoted in the West). You then divide these numbers by their "Impressing the Whites" quotient: Arundhati, 10; Kamala Das, 3; and Kiran Nagarkar: 2. In this hypothetical example, Arundhati's ultimate score of 9.8 will sink far below Kiran Nagarkar's 20, and not more than two "white-impressing" authors might make it into your list of ten. Now is your opportunity to make a courageous choice! Empower eight Indian authors who have *not* impressed the whites. And have no regrets, because 98 out of 100 Indian readers will in any case continue their slavish habits of buying *only* authors who have impressed the whites.

Fifth: Besides money, it is sex, Scotch, and scholarship — author Khushwant Singh's magical triumvirate of passions — that draw many of us to the West. Speaking of Scotch, India has a sizeable population of Scotch-drinkers or whiskey-drinking would-be Scotch drinkers, especially among the opinion-making classes. In their eyes, India's inability to make Scotch whiskey that is even a fraction as good as the original is the devastatingly conclusive proof of the superiority of Western civilization. The very day that India begins to make better Scotch than Scotland, better even than the Macallan and at a cheaper price, the population of our Firangophiles or Anglophiles would plunge by 50 percent. It is not impossible, I think. The draft beer served in Bangalore pubs is better than most American beer, though it has a long way to go to catch up with German and Czech beer. About sex and scholarship, I leave it to my elder colleague and expert Khushwant Singh to make suggestions.

Sixth: Foreign scholarships, medical residencies, advanced degrees, and jaunts abroad at any cost and for any purpose have become so hopelessly powerful to the urban Indian psyche that young sons-of-yuppies dream of an American education even before they have lost their first milk tooth. While an obvious reason for this attraction is superior career prospects and easy access to gadgets, an equally crucial if less obvious component is the lure of sexual freedom and erotic opportunity in the West — real or mythical. A possible cure for this (though I know some will say, "This is India, it won't work, yaar!"), even as an ideal to work for, gradually (as in Khushwant Singh's columns): Free our women's sexuality. Make a list of every repressive element that now restricts an individual woman's right to sexual knowledge, sexual pleasure, sexual laughter, nonsexual flirting, companionship, friendly touching, and relaxation, and slowly, gently, and cunningly relax these restrictions. If sex brings us to life, and if sex has been medically proven to have terrific health and emotional benefits, how can we unthinkingly import MTV and air-conditioned luxury cars, while damning sex as un-Indian?

This goal cannot be achieved with absolute success, I know, because democracy allows individuals or communities to resist change, seduction, and propaganda. But even if only 25 percent of these objectives are achieved for 25 percent of Indian women, India will be a completely different country. Once this Himalayan barrier to our happiness, sanity, and all-round mental balance is removed (and this holds good for the other South and West Asian countries too), we will not need to think, dream, or go West to fulfill our basic needs (when you Indian bureaucrats talk of "basic needs," have you ever considered this one?). Oh, yes, and let us not forget to educate our young men to become equal to the demands of these newly aroused and awakened young women — or we'll have hell to pay.

Seventh: Let us establish Decoconutification Centers, modeled on Detoxification Centers, to reeducate those who acquired their coconut mindsets along with their mother's milk.

Eighth: Let the entire thinking world community, not excluding those liberals who regard themselves as non-racist, consider long-term measures to reduce racial prejudice. One is to encourage interracial dating and marriage with grants of cash and subsidized housing, so that one day many of us will have relatives who are "mixed" — or more multi-racially evolved than the rest of us. Another is to encourage interracial adoptions, with similar incentives, so that many a couple will have one dark-skinned child and one light-skinned child. What a fine solution that will be to the problem of declining fertility rates in Western countries and the simultaneous problems of war orphans and overpopulation in non-Western countries.

Nine: This is the only mildly white-approved suggestion. Raimon Panikkar, in his engaging and powerful book *Cultural Disarmament: The Way of Peace* suggests that most cultures are traditionally aggressive, designating other cultures as enemies, barbarians, goys, mlecchas, kafirs, pagans, infidels and the like. He proposes "cultural disarmament," meaning a cessation of such hostile attitudes to other cultures. He also admits that for this to happen, cultures and people need to start from a position of equality. In other words, unilateral disarmament on the part of the weaker cultures could quite possibly result in their extinction. The initiative for disarmament has to come from the stronger cultures. Meanwhile, it will not be a bad idea to empower the weaker cultures with a little laughter, and the tongue-in-cheek lines in this book are intended as my tiny contribution to that goal.

Ten: I repeat. Compulsory universal multiple citizenship of at least three countries, one of these by birth or choice, and two allotted by lottery, with at least one being a major developing country, is an idea that will dilute the worst excesses of nationalism, and tend to distribute resources more fairly. It won't be easy to implement, and seems so daring and cheeky as to sound like fantasy, but so were many of the ideas proposed a hundred years ago, which are now an integral part of the way we live. And until its actual implementation, how about a non-governmental organization actually taking the initiative to allot honorary citizenships of two other countries to everyone who is presently restricted to one (a few countries already permit dual citizenship, which is a good thing).

* * *

Finally, Indians, like their Third World fellowmen, must take a long-term view (our yugas, or ages, run for billions of years, after all — after which the cycle repeats itself), exercise patience, and in the meanwhile, try to retain their dignity. Read the stoics, especially *The Meditations* of Marcus Aurelius. When you are going to be weak for a long, long time anyway, you might as well make a virtue of weakness (while secretly preparing for your ultimate victory). Remind yourselves that the barbarians overcame the Romans, the North Vietnamese defeated the French and the Americans; your time will come.

NO MORE CULTURAL SUBSERVIENCE

If you've come this far, then you are tough as nails, and an intelligent reader. You can take it. Fasten your seatbelts, then.

One of the most legendary acts of literary rebellion against the Not-So-New-White-World-Order was a novel called *Native Son* written by the black American writer Richard Wright. How important is this book? I quote:

"The day *Native Son* appeared," writes Irving Howe, "American culture was changed forever." *Native Son* shattered the myth that the descendants of slaves were "patient or forgiving. A blow at the white man, the novel forced him to recognize himself as an oppressor. A blow at the black man, the novel forced him to recognize the cost of his submission." — *Books of The Century*, ed. Elizabeth Diefendorf, Oxford University Press, 1996.

This is the intent of my book: to force the nonwhite man, at the beginning of the Twenty-first century, to recognize the cost of his submission. For those readers still unconvinced of this cost to their integrity as human beings, and also for those readers who need a white-skinned authority to be persuaded, I shall provide one. The British writer Ian Buruma, in his brilliant book of essays on various Asian societies, *The Missionary and The Libertine: Love and War in the East and the West*, accuses the urban upper classes of the Phillippines of "giving head" to various foreign conquerors, while it was the lower classes and the rural tribes who maintained their dignity and fought for freedom.

This powerful charge of Buruma's hit me so hard, because I immediately recognized elements of the same behavior in India's upper and Westernized classes. I saw, in retrospect, that my "criticism" of India's Christian community in *The Revised Kama Sutra* had partly been a commentary on its subservience or indirect collaboration with the British before India's independence, its having given the British more adulation and flattery by imitation per capita than most other Indian communities. But in the fifty years since independence, the Christian community, nowadays far more nationalistic and conscientious than its ancestors (and always less amenable to bribery and corruption than the mainstream), has been overtaken by India's yuppie, mostly-Hindu urban elite (including some successful Indo-Anglian writers), now the chief suppliers of the same commodity to the West. Indeed, you will find more Indian values, Indian hospitality and warmth, and Indian customs among India's rural Christians (those from Kerala, Karnataka, Tamil Nadu, and some Northeastern states) than among this Westernized urban elite.

Even if one is doing it oneself, one is often unconscious of it, and the shock of the naming, like a particularly brutal insight coming from a courageous psychoanalyst, must make us pause and reconsider. I leave it to you to decide whether Anglophilia, which afflicts a large number of Indians in varying degrees, may be designated as a subclass of this phenomenon, or whether it could be categorized a simple, innocuous preference or avocation, such as a passion for collecting stamps, or for gardening. Perhaps the matter bears discussion. But there is no doubt that its occurrence must make the British dance in their pin-striped suits, thanks to a simple natural law: how can you not love those who worship you? And if the British love it — and the British still flex far more muscle than you think[18] — then Anglophilia is bound to pay, just as a nice pre-milking massage to a cow is bound to pay in extra milk.

Examine some of the success stories among Indian writers, and

---

[18] It has just been revealed that they can spy on every e-mail communication or cellular phone call in the world, the Worldwide Web now being revealed as the CIA-OSS-Spy Web.

you notice that the common thread that connects Niradh Chaudhuri, Amitav Ghosh, and Pankaj Mishra is their Anglophilia. Indian Anglophilia, as I've observed it, is full of pathos, of longing for a lost time, a lost beauty, a lost order. In its more sympathetic forms, this affliction manifests itself in individuals who try to recall or reconstruct the glorious Days of Empire in the decrepit buildings of today's Calcutta. In its ridiculous forms, it is seen in the character of Bag in the novel *The Revised Kama Sutra:* her daily act of solidarity with the British, whose premature departure from India she mourns, is to lay a turd in a tin can. However superficially different their class and sophistication, Bag and Pankaj are siblings under the skin.

Some might argue that the action of a major Indian newspaper, whose management some years back told its then-literary editor that "there will be no more book reviews of *Indian* authors except for Shobha De" [the review section would mainly review foreign, meaning Western, books], falls in this category of giving head to Western civilization. Can you imagine the uproar if *The New York Times Book Review* were to announce that in future, it would review only British and Indian authors, and no American authors except for Jackie Collins?

Since Westerners are not that easily accessible to most ordinary Indians, Indians sometimes "give head" to the local brown-skinned Viceroys appointed by the West. A beautiful reporter once interviewed me in Delhi just after the publication of my second book, *Beauty Queens, Children, and the Death of Sex.* The interview went just splendidly, except for one strange question-answer statement by the interviewer, which I ignored: "What do you think of Arundhati Roy? I hope you are not saying anything against her, because we all love her." A few weeks later, I was surprised to read a derogatory and satirical printed interview, with invented dialogue and heavy judgment, and only a faint resemblance to what had actually transpired. This rape of journalistic ethics was obviously her revenge, her method of giving head to the West, for my perceived slights to its lawfully appointed Vicereine.

But it is not just upper class Indians in India who do it. Indian writers in the West also do it, by scrupulously grazing within the territorial limits imposed on them, and by too easily bashing 'desi' Indian males to appease Western feminists (who are extremely powerful in publishing), as in the numerous recent nonwhite (including Afro-American) novels with male characters who are monsters and in the obviously ingratiating answer made by one Indian woman writer at a conference, when asked who her audience was: "I write for women and intelligent men." That this pays handsomely is evident. Pankaj Mishra, having scorned and shown disgust towards non-upper-class Indian males for having sex on their minds, was recently *rewarded* with a handsome advance for *The Romantics,* a novel that Indian reviewers have been lukewarm towards.

But great advances do not equal great writing or great art. Cervantes, Poe, Chester Himes, the Chinese poet Du Fu, all died poor or struggled financially at some point in their lives rather than sell themselves — not that they didn't need or want money, but that there was a certain point beyond which they refused to prostitute their art. Picasso died rich, but in his art (as well as in his dealings with women) he was a law unto himself. Can we not at least try the path of integrity for a while? I suggest: let all Asian writers — all without exception, from Rushdie to the smallest fry who managed to get his or her mug into the *New Yorker* or some such Western organ — at least for one year, starting from April 1, 2000, try to write completely outside the permitted territory. No doubt, for the sake of their bread and butter, they will have to return to writing the usual pandering pap from April 1, 2001, and for the rest of their lives; but for one year, just one trial year on behalf of their dignity, I call on all Asian writers to rebel against their colonial destiny, even if that means sacrificing a few delicious Western perks for a while (and ditto to other nonwhite authors). I also call upon prominent Indian writers and editorialists to speak out publicly (and even you, my Elder Brother Salman), expressing their opposition to any suppression or step-motherly treatment to any brave book by any Indian author.

While many of their colleagues may have compromised themselves by brownnosing the powerful for too long, I ask every ethical and courageous reporter who interviews these writers in the future to put this question to them: Are you willing to stand up for a fellow Indian writer, and to protest proven or reasonably obvious cases of suppression or censorship of courageous Indian voices? If these writers are not willing to raise their voices, and if we hold the Vichy government of World War II France to be guilty of collaboration for having looked the other way while Jews were being sent to the camps, then they will be similarly guilty of collaboration with the White Apartheid Establishment.

Above all, let all of the members of India's upper classes take the following solemn oath: *No More Head!* We have to come to a consensus that we won't give head. It has to be on the national agenda, it has to be discussed in academic conferences, in colloquia organized by the Sahitya Akademi and the Ministry of Culture (and its Department of No Head Enforcement), as well as by major national magazines and newspapers. The culture of giving head, or literary, artistic, commercial, political, and cultural prostitution by nonwhite countries, is so pervasive and unconscious that even decent people do it without thinking of it as such. It is time to name this evil, to call it by its true name, rather than, by fearing the words, to continue to practice that which we haven't fully admitted. For why should white writers like Ian Buruma and Henry Miller have a monopoly in not fearing words, while we, fearing them, are oppressed by them? And if this requires the creation of a 12-Step society called Head-Givers Anonymous, so be it. I am sure we can get a few Filipino and other Third World brothers to join in and provide us with expert advice.

Why can Kancha Ilaiah, author of *Why I Am Not a Hindu,* and Swapan K. Biswas, author of *Gods, False Gods, and the Untouchables* summon up rare courage in their writings? And why do I rate them higher than certain other celebrated writers? Because to have been an untouchable or a sudra (low-caste person) in India is to have been trampled on so much that you have nothing more to fear. That Occidentals do not read such writers is their loss. These are the real Indians.

A POLITICAL CORRECTNESS PRIMER FOR
WHITE PEOPLE
How to Behave Towards Browns

I cannot pretend that this book is *not* going to have Western readers. Indeed, though I mainly address an Indian and Third World audience, Westerners might ironically form the majority of my readership. This chapter is therefore addressed to them, for it takes both Impressors and Impressees to play this game, which is an act of collusion from both sides. And whites, being the Impressees, can greatly help in putting an end to this masquerade.

So you are the decent, noble, liberal, fair-minded Westerner (like my Western friends), and this book has not put you to sleep, but has shocked and upset you, and perhaps even (I am being optimistic here) opened your eyes. So what do you do to correct your unconscious prejudice, so far disastrous to all but a minority of Indians and Third Worlders? And how do you change a world, a large proportion of whose inhabitants are now in the position of being circus monkeys performing for a few white patrons?

First: As a general rule, the more British or American the accent of an Asian person, the more skeptical you ought to be of her claims to authenticity, for it is quite likely that she has uncritically imbibed Western prejudices, or has learned to provide the right kind of fish bait to the Western fishes she now lives among. Unless, you prefer precisely the company of such Indians: being that they are your creations, your bambinos! In which case, pet them, please.

Second: Remember that there is a class system in India and most Asian countries, and that the fact that certain individuals went to Oxford or Cambridge means that they were merely the best among an economically and socially privileged few. It is even possible that they were simply the brightest or the pushiest among the 0.2 percent of the urban children whose parents were rich, motivated, or well-connected enough to afford to send them to good schools in India, in order to consider the possibility of sending them abroad.

Recognize, too, that these Show Indians, who have spent years refining their act and cultivating their patrons, oppress many other more-Real Indians to protect their operation (this is the real story *The New Yorker* should spend a year investigating, for far less than the cost of flying twelve authors to London for a group photograph). Therefore, their opinions may not be free of prejudice. If an anti-establishment Indian writer were to send a letter to PEN American Center's president, for example, and the president were to consult with an Establishment Indian writer on the letter's veracity, it would be like consulting a Chinese police chief on the authenticity of an allegation of brutality at Tiananmen Square.

Westerners who reside in India and who, unlike the few missionaries and idealists, live the high life in its cosmopolitan cities, know that the price of being chummy with India's upper crust (its democratic and creative maharajahs) and of enjoying their hospitality is to wink at their oppressions of the lower classes — and, in fact, to participate in those oppressions. You have no such incentive to do so.

Third: If you are a publisher, you could set aside 50 percent of your "brown boys" budget for non-Oxbridge and non-Ivy League and non-upper-class Indian writers. What? You gave it all away to Pankaj Mishra?! [an Indian author who received a $400,000 advance for a hyped but disappointing novel.]. If Knopf and the big boys refuse to go along, as is quite likely, you could then set aside 75 percent of that budget to correct the imbalance. And be sure you set aside at least half of your "brown boys" budget for *boys*, not girls; reverse discrimination may help you ease your guilt about your own past, but it causes ridiculous posturing, injustice, and dissension among those on whom this discrimination is imposed. It simply does not make sense that some brown man in a small Indian town should pay for the past "sexist" "sins" of the privileged white males who continue to be privileged because they continue to be your lovers, husbands, fathers, and brothers.

Fourth: When a well-connected Indian writer, a Good Old Boy (GOB) named Pankaj Mishra, read the manuscript of Arundhati Roy's novel, he didn't get in touch with the editor-in-chief of Penguin India, or any other fellow-brownskinned editor. Without a moment's pause, he phoned his friend David Gordon, the London literary agent. It was like making a long-distance call to God, rather than to some lowly assistant padre or one-winged angel. In a matter of months, so many zillions of dollars were cascading into Roy's bank account that the bank was demanding paramilitary commando protection. No Indian editor would have managed to pony up even a meager two thousand dollars (the usual advance is two hundred fifty dollars), and in all likelihood, this pittance, with typical Indian efficiency, would have been collapsed into her account, minus the usual collection fees and taxes, a year later. The message for Indians: *A white man can be your savior, but never a brown man. Don't even dream of wasting your energy on a fellow brown person. The moment you see a brown man approach, run in the opposite direction.*

This is a terribly depressing and demoralizing state of affairs for Indians and Third World people: the thought that their salvation rests not in themselves or their fellow countrymen, but in people with pale complexions. No wonder Christianity is catching on in the East, even as it is declining in the West (Prime Minister Vajpayee, sound the alarm bells, and ask the bhaiyyas to start writing large royalty checks to their authors in lieu of the donations they are making to your party funds!). What can you, as a rich white liberal and non-proselytizer, do if the spectacle of once-blissful savages kneeling mournfully before a Christian Cross outrages you? Contribute to a rainforest program or carry a "green" credit card to assuage your guilt? No. Instead, encourage or even invest in independent Third World publishing, establishing high-class writing programs and arts colonies in the Third World, and giving direct grants to individual writers, without demanding any political or editorial control, except the assurance that the money is being properly spent and is going to independent writers. Given the thesis of this book, it is quite likely that you will act at least five decades before Indians, now busy building temples and buying Mercedeses, will wake up to the importance of this.

Since art, independence, self-confidence, and world peace are so inextricably linked, this is as important a task as, say, sending money for Third World development projects. Hitler became Hitler primarily because he had an inferiority complex, and a sense of injustice. So stop thinking of this as charity, or wondering why rich Indians don't help their own (they won't, they're too busy aping you, often in your worst aspects, they are the parodies of your worst class of people); you are helping a fellow human being, and above all, you are helping yourselves. The benefits of helping independent writers may be less screamingly obvious than those of sending money to OXFAM or UNICEF; you won't notice formerly thin but laughing naked children now solemnly weighed down by their ill-fitting shorts and their heavy school books. But by helping brave writers to thrive, to rise up and rebel (and if necessary, to curse you), you will have done something to help reduce the slavish and fearful mentality that hobbles our dynamism and our progress.

Fifth: Those of you who wish to aspire to a higher standard of non-racism than you have achieved until now, please submit to the following test:

How many nonwhite persons have you:

a) Invited to your homes?

b) Had friendships with over long periods?

c) Helped for no reason or personal benefit whatsoever?

d) Had as clients — clients who can give positive notes about these experiences, when asked in confidence?

If you answered, "Not a single one" to more than two of these questions, you may be guilty of racism by default. Please embark on some corrective measures, now.

Also, consider this. "You're Indian! Then you should be a Hindu!" many a Westerner will say to an Indian Christian, immediately obliterating the existence of 30 million Indian Christians. India's

Hindus know that Westerners want their exotica simple and uncomplicated, so that they should shove their Christian citizens under their Hindoo rugs in order to market their brand most profitably. So do émigré Hindus, who rarely will include an Indian Christian on their cultural committees, lest the whites think them not authentically Indian — and the West plays along

Refuse to accept a simplistic, generalized understanding of India or the East; do not tolerate those who will pander to your ignorance, your prejudices, or your taste for the exotic.

Sixth: Until things change, let's dispense with the hypocrisy. Have Disney World change its theme song to "It's a White World After All!"

Seventh: The ultimate cure, as James Baldwin noted, is not a few condescending gestures from above. The ultimate cure is to give up at least some of your power, for power is what the powerless need to feel less like pawns and more like masters of their own destiny. Power is not just the media, but the media is a good start, because the media controls the mind, and as Dan Quayle might have said, what a waste it is not to own even your own mind. Perhaps the William Gates Foundation could buy a couple of large publishing houses, newspapers, and perhaps even a television channel and hand them over to card-holding members of a proposed group called CON: Committee of Non-Coconuts. Why non-coconuts? Because it would be pointless to hand over a publishing company to a brown person who thinks exactly like you: you'll be simply producing more imitative Jane Austenish novels of manners peopled by exotic Hindoo characters whose insides have been marinated with the correct spices. Indeed, before you do any kind of handing over, please, please, submit the person you are handing it over to a lie-detector test, and a coconut-detector test which shows that the person has a history of being independent, risking poverty and rejection rather than their integrity.

PREFACE TO THE FIRST EDITION (2000)
THE TWO WORLDS

President Bill Clinton tells Indian Prime Minister Vajpayee, minutes after meeting him on his first visit to India, "Hey, Vaj baby, I've got to talk to you about Pack-i-Stan and the bomb."

And Vajpayee replies, "No, Bill bhai. First of all, I want you to read these two books by Richard Crasta. I have an Avro HS-748 waiting to fly you to a deserted island in the Andamans, so you can concentrate. And remember: the first subject on the agenda when you return is the chapter in his book, *Impressing the Whites*: Monica Lewinsky's Thong Underwear."

Fifteen minutes later, Bill Clinton, who in a daze has opened the package right there in Vajpayee's presence and started reading it, is rolling on the floor laughing, while the Secret Service surrounds him, mistaking his behavior to be the first symptoms of some strange new deadly poison slipped into his welcome drink. And Bill Clinton finally recovers from his laughter and tells Vajpayee, pointing to the title, *Impressing the Whites*, "Precisely the book my Secretary of State asked me to bring along as a gift for you."

Only a few days later, Bill Gates decides to build a $500 million second home in India, of which he is also now a citizen. The walls are hung not with digital masterpieces, but with live Indians, their bodies painted for less than the cost of the expensive art that usually hangs on billionaires' walls.

To celebrate this change in the zeitgeist, Abraham Lincoln dances a jig in his grave and howls with laughter.

White people walk around dazed, telling each other, "Have you read that book yet?" And everybody knows exactly which book they are talking about. All over the country and the world, people in the highest walks of life hold seminars on the book and its meaning, and policy changes are being announced every second. The familiar faces in the newspapers are replaced by newer faces: darker faces. *Rambo V: First Spinning Wheel* stars an Rambo who goes on a fast unto death to protest cruelty to mosquitoes. However, since he has plenty of fat to burn, he decides in the meanwhile to test his will power by sleeping with naked Viet Cong guerillas.

Obviously, the above scenario is a bhang-induced dream, and this book, which discloses the one guaranteed formula for success in today's world, may not even get a fraction of one percent of the attention of the high-living crowd. So what? During my last two months in India, thanks to an extremely light schedule (no television crews waiting outside my heavily guarded gate for sound bites, no London superagents banging on my door and making me miserable), I have been meeting all the right people. The unemployed, part-time working mothers, Dalit poets and writers, a bank clerk trying to rent a flat in Bangalore, those for whom *Delhi dur ast*–for whom Delhi is far away.

And what I have discovered (or rediscovered) is that there are two Indias; the one that rules, and the one that is ruled. Similarly, there are two Worlds: the one that rules, and the one that is ruled.

The latter world includes a young writer named Rod, who said to me, while advising me on the 48-page booklet that was the precursor of this book: "Don't weaken it! Every time you edit it, you weaken it. Don't compromise!" There is the Indian mother and part-time editor in Bangalore who said to me (I had been anxious that I had gone too far): "Don't apologize! It's embarrassing when you apologize! Someone needs to say this!"

So if the Rulers are a little uneasy, and don't quite respond in the fantastic way depicted in the first paragraph of this book; and if the Other India, and the Other World, is delighted . . . what is a writer to do? Nothing, except keep on doing the job he was meant to do. My karma, or my fate, is to write in plain language, and to reach the kind of people who would fall asleep in the middle of a sentence of Ashis

Nandy's or that of the other brainy intellectuals most would-be intellectuals spend their nights cramming.

To me, there's no point speaking about the Other India, or the Other World, if that world cannot understand what I am saying. That is why I decided at the last moment, after having long dropped the idea, that the book would indeed be decorated by the cartoons of Sailesh, an Invisible Artist from rural South Kanara—an artist who would be too lowbrow for most intellectuals, who are too mentally constipated to laugh (until enough Nobel Prizes or Bookers are given to comic writers, or they learn that Edward Albee admitted that the film comedians Abbott and Costello have been a profound influence on his work).

There may after all be many in the Other India for whom *my* words, and my long sentences, are constipating; and Sailesh's pictures may speak to them eloquently. It is for this other world, and this other India that this book is primarily written for.

But I won't complain if this book were indeed read by the First World: the world that rules. At one point, during the checkered history of this book's writing and publication, an audio-biography of Abraham Lincoln had inspired me to continue, despite the troublesome questions I wished to hide from. For it was then that I realized that my book's main theme was an amplification and modernization of Abraham Lincoln's chief message. On today's shrunken planet with its outmoded nation-states, "A nation divided against itself cannot stand" has become "A humanity divided against itself cannot stand."

EPILOGUE: THE AFTERMATH

Impressing the Whites took me 1.5 of my best years to write, and approximately another six months to publish, promote, and sell — and it earned me around four thousand dollars over the next ten years, or one-fortieth of the value of my time, considering that when I wrote it, I was living in the U.S. and had two American Masters' Degrees, one from a top university.

Nobody *told* me to write that book (to answer a question from an idiotic Delhi wine salesman-cum-con-man, who petulantly asked me, "Who *told* you to become a writer?"). I wrote it for a simple reason, and for the only reason that true writers write (or so I hope) — it came from my heart, and had I not done all in my power to write it and give it to the world, I would have lost respect for myself, and I would have lost my soul.

I still believe that no other Indian publisher would have dared to publish it word for word. Indeed, one former friend and fan of the book said to me, "If you had given it to a regular publisher, it would have ended up as a 2-page book: The Acknowledgments Page, and the Dedication Page." So I did it myself (and that's my answer to *The Hindu* and all those snotty Indian newspapers who dishonestly tried to throttle its revolutionary message with the claim that it was *self*-published: yes, like Walt Whitman's *Leaves of Grass,* for example, or James Joyce's *Ulysses,* or Proust's *Remembrance of Things Past*).

Yes, I did it at my cost, and knowing that far graver than the financial risk involved was the massive risk to my literary career, and my future prospects; I said "To Hell with it!" and published it anyway.

Strangely the book, though written with mega-idealistic intent, escaped the radars of the liberals and their fellow idealists, thanks to India's efficient Ayatollah machine, run both by liberals and by devout, semi-literate businessmen who read little and understand little except money. And why should that have surprised me? The book was exposing the racket that millions of Indians, including some of our literary idols (Arundhati Roy included), were making millions at. Whether you agree or disagree with this thesis, you must grant that I make my case over the course of a nearly-200- page book, and that at least 1,500 readers (and possibly up to 10,000, given the way books are passed around in India), including a BBC country chief and a Singapore editor/publisher (who bought Singapore regional rights from me) have found this case quite compelling.

And if you disagree with the book, you ought to respond to it rationally and with fair argument, instead of by suppressing the book with dishonesty and dirty tactics.

Far worse than being ignored, I was being *punished* by the liberal Indian literary establishment for *Impressing the Whites,* which disappeared from Indian bookshelves after briefly being a Delhi bestseller, some of its initial supporters spinelessly turning on me after being chastised by their more unabashedly Ayatollah-ish friends (yes, the liberal Ayatollahs — who would have imagined this strange marriage of fascism with upper-class liberals!).

I spent the next ten years in the literary wilderness, formerly lionized, but now completely out of India's bookstores — until the HarperCollins India edition of *The Revised Kama Sutra* was published in September 2010, with one-twentieth of the fanfare of books that it was ten times as good as (a book launch in Bangalore was attended mostly by thrill-seeking celebrity f***ers who were there to see the Chief Guest, the Lokayukta of Karnataka, was followed by a book launch in a small bookshop in a remote corner of Delhi mainly attended by the Managing Director and his buddies). Yes, it's back to the wilderness again, I've not heard of the book and its sales since publication.

During those ten years in the wilderness, there were two other occasions when I summoned my failing courage and made attempts at defiance — *What We All Need* in 2005 and *The Killing of an Author* in 2007/2008 — the latter, a book whose anti-Establishment balls are equal to those of *Impressing the Whites*. Both were crushed with greater efficiency than *Impressing the Whites* had been (while *Impressing the Whites* received national media coverage — though some of it dishonest — and display in at least 50 bookstores nationwide, the latter two books never made it to more than ten of over five thousand Indian bookstores), I found myself stretched for an extended period on the rack of poverty and debt.

At this point, the desperate need for survival at all costs had taken its toll on my former independence and fearlessness. I started to censor my writings post-2005, deleting many of my fiery blog posts or toning them down endlessly to prevent giving offence to the readers who might possibly help me with a meal by buying a single copy of a book.

Indeed, I began to gag myself and to do the very thing I had criticized: to follow the Ninth Commandment of Impressing the Whites ("Behave yourself!") in the hope that the Indian Literary Establishment (a subsidiary of the Western establishment) and the far wealthier Western literary establishment itself would forgive me my former defiance and give me the royalty advances that would help me recover some sense of selfhood.

But after three years of doing this off and on, and with every hoped for mega-carrot turning out to be an illusory carrot or a baby carrot, I learned the lesson: that I never had, and never would be forgiven for *Impressing the Whites* and the subsequent *The Killing of an Author*, unless I surrendered all of my manhood and became a craven slave.

Which I never, never will be.

At a moment when I am in debt, and face so many restrictions on my life, and am nearly powerless, it gives me great pleasure to return *Impressing the Whites* to its proper place — the public space, where it breathed only briefly, before being throttled or condemned to a dungeon, where it has spent most of the last ten years. And I hope that this time around, it will receive the discussion and the fair reading that it never received the first time.

What you see before you is chiefly the 2000 edition along with minor revisions made for the 2002 edition; only the example of David Davidar was added post-2002 to illustrate one of the Commandments — I have not done any deep thinking about this book since then, and cannot say what I would write if I were to write the book today — or even whether I would write it at all, though I strongly suspect, as the French say, that the more things change, the more they stay the same (or, as the famous song says, "The fundamental things apply, as time goes by"). And as I have many other new books in progress, desperately competing for my attention, I don't plan to rethink the subject at length unless commissioned to do so with a fair advance or grant. For now, I only return to the public what was unfairly stolen from them by the Ayatollahs, and leave it up to them to see what they can find in it. Surely there is some rethinking to be done, especially as the world has become more multiracial and more multiracial children are being born (and I am happy with this phenomenon); the phenomenon of President Barack Obama, whose election I strongly supported, also needs to be factored in. But I cannot do it at present, and for now, as my former British agent had said of *The Revised Kama Sutra*: *It is what it is.*

Also, as this book, edited in 2002, had to be suppressed for eight years, and not see the light of day; and as I do not have the time to go through this book and rethink every sentence in it, I have decided simply to give retrospective freedom of expression to the Richard Crasta who was suppressed in 2002, and to let his long-imprisoned 2002 edition see the light of day. So please take this as a book from a moment in time (and all books are exactly that: books written at a moment in time), and enjoy what you relish and what resonates with you, and reject what does not.

I appeal to those who have a tendency to crush writers whose opinions they disagree with: Please respect the Spirit of Independence and Freedom that speaks through me and that gives me courage; do not respect me for specific words that came through my pen and that you agreed with (or spurn me for those you disagreed with, for who knows that I may disagree with them myself, once the words have escaped my pen). Respect me and nurture me rather for the persistence and dedication that makes me keep writing, and writing, and writing what I feel to be the truth, even when I have lost nearly everything I ever had, including the fame and celebrity I could have easily clung to and milked forever by playing safe thereafter and embracing and *becoming* the Establishment.

Those who wish to see a newer edition, or an edition that is brought up to date, will have to await such a time as I receive adequate support from a sponsor, and meanwhile, send me their comments or opinions to rc@richardcrasta.com with "Impressing the Whites — comments" in the subject line. Meanwhile, a request to readers that they approach established Western publishers urging them to publish a Western paperback edition of the book, or even a post-Obama-ist edition of the book.

ENDNOTES

Colonial chic: Does the recent fashion and surfeit of colonial names, especially the ones with phallic overtones, represent the sexual undertones of colonialism, as hinted at in the definition of "Octerlony Monument" in the glossary of *The Revised Kama Sutra*? Is the new triumvirate: Peter Scot, Peter England, and Penguin India (founded by Peter Mayer)? Has the long arm of the law become the long dick of imperialism? Does the stiff upper lip signify a stiff lower organ? Is this thirst for British dickie symbolic of the complex longing of the violated (colony) for the violating colonizer's sword?

Delhi's Western Diplomats: For example, the agency that is most powerful in the literary life of Delhi is not any Indian organization, or even India's Ministry of Information and Broadcasting. It is the British Council. If you want to launch a book and get the maximum attention and sales in Delhi, get the British Council to do your book launch for you. The book sells itself on the snob appeal, to the people who have banged on the doors and impressed their way into this Anglican cathedral of High Taste, and now want to show off their "taste" and literary seriousness to their fellow snobs; then, the very fact that two hundred or so of the "right people" have bought it has a snowballing effect for the book's sales.

So Colin Perchard, the director of British Council in Delhi, can easily call himself Pasha Perchard. For it is he who certifies who is Indian and who is not, who is literary and who is not. When I called him about possibly launching of the memoirs of my father, a former soldier in the British Indian Army (and later, the Indian Army), he disposed of the case in two minutes with a snooty, "Oh, I don't think we would be interested in doing the book of an NRI." He was technically correct: my father had died two months earlier, and in his deceased state, could no longer strictly be called a resident of India, even though he *had* been one while alive.

It was ironic, though, that fifty years after India's independence from Britain, a representative of India's former colonial masters was certifying whether a person was an Indian or a Non-Resident Indian, and that this certification nearly made the difference between life and death (in a literary manner of speaking) for the person concerned.

Consider the reverse: What if Colin Perchard happened to be an Indian named Kalidas Pasha heading the Indian Arts Council in London or in Washington? He would then just be one of a hundred cultural ambassadors doing their shtick, lucky if he got a few minutes of airtime once a year. He would certainly not rule the cultural life of London or Washington (the way Colin Perchard presently did). Neither would the editor of Rupa Books, India, dictate the name of the next American writer to have a bestselling book (the way British publishers now managed to dictate which Indian writers would become bestselling authors). How unequal the relative power of our two countries, how stupid and craven we Indians must be to *give* them, our former colonial masters, this power!

One must acknowledge that this power can and is often used for good, as in making information available to hungry native minds; but like any instrument, power can be used for good or bad. Are we so naïve as to believe that the existence of such enormous foreign power in our cultural life does not stifle or crush dissent, its presence sometimes functioning like a birth control pill that prevents the very act of conception or snuffs out the idea or the embryo shortly after conception?

Impressing, culinary division: Even ten-percent-nonwhite countries like Greece dress up to impress the High White races such as the Germans; you can go through a breakfast buffet at a Rhodes hotel and leave with nothing but the taste of sausage and bread and cheese of different kinds. You can bet the people of Rhodes wouldn't have anything to do with that food if the choice were theirs. As

America exports its Hiltons, Holiday Inns, and Sheratons, their extraordinary ability to suck the last milligram of taste out of any kind of cuisine whatsoever is simultaneously absorbed by the locals. In a country like India, where unemployed labor is cheap and begging to be employed, it is nearly impossible to find a pot of freshly brewed leaf tea anymore, and the labor-saving, flavor-killing tea bag has become a badge of modernity and progress with which the locals hope to impress the whites and be adopted for the membership of some new international trade organization.

Suzanne Arundhati Roy: A friend, a Keralite who claims to have met Arundhati Roy's mother Mary Roy, told me her original name was Margaret Roy. Which turned out to be erroneous, as he may have substituted the "Suzanne" for Margaret. But the truth of this matter doesn't really interest me (except to the extent that I reported it in an earlier edition, which I regret). *Even if she did change her name, that's her personal choice, and she has every right to choose any name she wishes, whatever her reason, and regardless of the religion she practices or does not practice.* What I am really interested in is the perception — nay, the conviction — of the people who told me this story, and of others presented with the theoretical possibility, that Arundhati Roy had ten times the chance of selling books in the West than Margaret Roy. And which Western literary agent would come out and solemnly swear on the Bible or the Torah that this is absolutely not and never was the case?

If the principle is true (whether or not the case of Roy is true), then the West does in fact dictate our identities, and even our religion. This is not to excuse the despicable caste-mindedness of some Indians, even those who think themselves liberal. For example, in my second book, an essay collection called *Beauty Queens, Children, and the Death of Sex,* I announced to the world (how much more public can one get than writing a book?), in a semi-satirical essay called "An Obituary for a Name," that I would change my name to "Avatar Prabhu" on August 15, 1997, the fiftieth anniversary of India's independence. It was a nuanced and satirical essay about identity, religion, colonialism, and modern marketing, which could provide enough material for discussion in a three-day seminar. But instead, the book, possibly because it contained other subversive material, has almost never been read or properly and fully read (especially by a few of the journalists who interviewed me about it, and reviewers who read it), and it has received many reactions of the potato-trader-who-wandered-into-publishing breed. The reaction, which astounded me, springs from a deep, despicable caste mentality whose underlying attitude may be summed up in this sentence: *How dare a Christian, a mere kafir who is not a Hindu by birth and caste, and can never be, take on a Hindu name?*

I am sure these people would similarly deride black poet LeRoi Jones for having changed his name to Amiri Baraka — thus simply negating or refusing to attempt to understand *the politics of protest* that motivated his decision. But then, I am wrong to be offended by the perceptions of the many uneducated, uncultured, and bigoted potato-and-onion traders who have wandered into Indian publishing and bookselling and own or manage at least half of it.

By the way, I never *actually* changed my name, and my decision not to go ahead with a legal name change proceeded from my unwillingness to associate myself with pseudo-religious fanatics and goons of any kind, some of whom have become communalist bigots. But curiously, my American part-time literary agent, who is far less established than my previous British agent, was able to sell translation rights for Avatar Prabhu to six foreign countries, whereas my British agent was unable to sell Richard Crasta to a single one other than to Fourth Estate. My soft and ambivalent answer: so long as this enables more people to *read* my 400-page novel, and so long as I am powerless to change the stupidity of the publishing world and its public relations machine, this is not a matter important enough to get worked up about.

A GLOSSARY FOR THE CONFUSED AND THE INNOCENT

"Bollywood" and "filmi": Bollywood is the jolly term given to the phenomenon called Bombay Hollywood, which mainly produces fantastic romantic musicals for India's masses. "Filmi" means "Bollywood-film-related."

brown: occasionally used as a general term for all nonwhite people and Asians. This is not meant to exclude other colors, and not even the few extremely fair-skinned persons of Asian descent, but for simplicity and sometimes for alliterative or linguistic effect. Politically correct terms such as "persons of color," unfortunately, are extremely inelegant, besides being not colorful enough.

Brown bad boys: In reality: troublesome minor thugs. Because of their genetic incompetence, they are incapable of evil on a grand scale as, say, Adolf Hitler and Genghis Khan were capable of.

Desi: An Indian without airs, naturally, unabashedly himself/herself. Derogatory and humorous terms used by the more cosmopolitan or elite class of browns to describe spitters, shitters, and roadside buffoons — or simply the Unredeemed brownskinned. See also: desiwallas.

Desiwallas: fellow desis. Desis being a comic and semi-contemptuous term Indians use for their own kind, especially those whom they consider to be country bumpkins.

Phoren: of foreign (non-Indian) origin.

Oriental: I refer to the definition given by *The Oxbridge English Dictionary*, the indispensable guide to colonists:

Oriental: (n) short, obliging person of either sex, usually a waiter or masseuse. Very short, very obliging, will do things your fat mother or your stiff-backboned wife will never dream of doing, and may get you blackballed from The Club if openly expressed. An outraged Oriental (or his mother or sister) is easily mollified with a little back-sheesh. Long exposure to the sun has rendered them usually a little yellow or dark-skinned, but the usual want of intelligence is more than made up for by sexual and servile intelligence.

Oriental (definition No. 2): There are two types of Orientals in the Western mind: a) Wild-Eyed Eastern Terrorists, untrustworthy, troublemaking, usually represented by A-rab or I-ranian types or other Islamic nationals.
b) Smiling Orientals: harmonious, well-behaved, or bright and hardworking, grateful as puppy dogs for your attention, ready and anxious to please you and take care of your every need, a type that finds its highest expression in East Asian air hostesses, Balinese and Thai men and women, and hardworking and nearly glamorous Indian women, or happy and grateful suitable boys writing high-minded literature. OED's advice: a) Kill the former. b) Feed the latter, but not so much that they become fat and lazy and arrogant.

Yellow Bad Boys: Invented the Walkman, therefore higher in the scale of competence than brown bad boys; also, more to be feared because of their technological intelligence, immense industry, and World War II exploits.

ACKNOWLEDGMENTS

The author wishes to acknowledge Sunney Tharappen for having been a friend and champion, Siddhartha and Kumar and Sujata Arunachalam for their hospitality and friendship, Veena Rao for her encouragement, to Nandita Agarwal for her suggestions, and for all the invisible people who have cheered him on and given him strength through a rocky career. He also thanks Aashish Singla, Sudhi Rao, and Amarnath Bantwal for their recent support.

The author is also grateful to Henry Louis Gates, Jr. for permission to quote from *Thirteen Ways from Looking at a Black Man*. An earlier version of the essay "How To Be An Invisible Author" appeared in *India Today*.

No thanks at all to the baldy from Chelsea/Greenwich Village who claimed to have helped edit the book while I was recovering from surgery in 2001, and extremely vulnerable, and who decamped with over a thousand dollars of my money. If this 2002 version is better than the 2000 original, the credit goes to me. If it is worse, or if I go bald on account of its negative effects, the blame rests entirely on Mr. Baldy.

ABOUT THE AUTHOR

Richard Crasta was born in Bangalore, India, grew up in Mangalore, and moved to America after working briefly in the Indian Administrative Service, where he (unconvincingly to himself or others) played judge, magistrate, and distributor of land to the landless, among other things. His first novel, conceived in the New York suburbs at the same time as his first child, was ironically titled "The Revised Kama Sutra: A Novel of Colonialism and Desire" and published by Viking Penguin India and then by Fourth Estate, UK. It received wide critical acclaim in India, where it was a brief bestseller; later, it was described as "very funny" by Kurt Vonnegut. It has been published in ten countries and in seven languages.

Richard's twelve books include fiction, nonfiction, essays, autobiography, humor, cultural and political critiques, and satire, and have been described as "exuberant," "courageous," "hilarious," and "boldly going where no Indian writer has gone before." He has been interviewed or written about in "The New York Times," BBC TV and radio, The Independent (UK), Indian national television channels, and elsewhere. His three best books, in his opinion—the ones that required the most courage, care, passion, and time--are *The Revised Kama Sutra*, *Impressing the Whites*, and *The Killing of an Author*. *The Mahatma, the Goats, and Young Cats* is the title of a recent collection of his best humor to date.

A New Yorker for most of his adult life, father of three children, and member of PEN America, he is now a world citizen-at-large in Asia. His inspirations include Saul Bellow and Henry Miller, Shakespeare, and Charles Dickens. His Indian roots have always inspired him, and provided much of the material for his writings.